A Soldier's Diary
South Africa
1899–1901

I'D BETTER EXPLAIN THIS IS A MOONLIGHT SCENE –
THEY ARE NOT GOING THROUGH A TUNNEL

A Soldier's Diary
South Africa
1899-1901

The Experiences of a N.C.O. of the
Hants. Regiment and 7th Mounted Infantry
during the Boer War

Murray Cosby Jackson

LEONAUR

A Soldier's Diary
South Africa
1899-1901
The Experiences of a N.C.O. of the
Hants. Regiment and 7th Mounted Infantry
during the Boer War
by Murray Cosby Jackson

First published under the title
A Soldier's Diary
South Africa 1899-1901

Leonaur is an imprint
of Oakpast Ltd

ISBN: 978-1-84677-914-5 (hardcover)
ISBN: 978-1-84677-913-8 (softcover)

http://www.leonaur.com

Publisher's Notes

In the interests of authenticity, the spellings, grammar and place names
used have been retained from the original editions.

The opinions of the authors represent a view of events in which he
was a participant related from his own perspective,
as such the text is relevant as an historical document.

The views expressed in this book are not necessarily
those of the publisher.

Contents

Original Publisher's Note

This volume reached the publisher's hands in the form of two large manuscript books, filled with rather faded handwriting and decorated here and there with pen and ink drawings made by the author "as he went along." The books, on examination, proved to be a straightforward and unvarnished account of the experiences of a non-commissioned officer during the great Boer War, compiled for the benefit of his family circle and with no idea of subsequent publication. (Indeed, the author will in all probability not know that his words have been put into print until he is able to re-read them on his South African homestead!)

The chronicle was inclined to be "rambling," it was not furnished with dates, and—as was to be expected in an account prepared solely for the amusement of near relatives—it dealt only with what actually happened to the writer, and ignored events, perhaps of more historical importance, in which he did not happen to take part. It was compiled very soon after the matters described in it occurred, and grew out of a *Diary* kept during the War which the author unfortunately lost before Peace was signed.

In preparing the book for general reading the Publisher was confronted with two alternatives. Either it could be carefully "edited" from colloquial into written English, supplied with elaborate commentaries and put into proper chronological order; or it could be left exactly as it was written, and reproduced as a "human document" for the interest of soldiers who took part in the War, of their relatives, and of the still wider class of the reading public who are interested in "what it feels like to be under fire," in the psychology of warfare. Rightly or wrongly the latter course has been chosen, and the book and its illustrations are given with no further alteration than a perhaps rather arbitrary division into chapters, and the omission (solely on account of certain technical difficulties of reproduction) of a very few of the sketches.

A word should be said here of the author's personality. Sergeant Jackson is a son of Lieutenant-Colonel Halkett Jackson, who was mentioned in despatches by Lord Roberts at Cabul and saw much active service in different parts of the Empire. In spite of the modesty of his narrative the reader experienced in military matters will probably guess (as was the case) that Sergeant Jackson served with distinction in South Africa. Indeed, he was on at least two occasions offered a commission.

Finally, lest his expressive illustrations should be subjected to an academic criticism which they were not expected to face, it should be mentioned that he has never had a drawing lesson in his life. It is hoped that, although the official histories and accounts of the South African war which have appeared are many and excellent, there may yet be room for this entirely unofficial and graphic narrative of some of that campaign's less-known phases.

Chronological Table of Principal Events in the Boer War

War Declared	Oct.11, 1899
Siege of Kimberley	,, 15, 1899
Talana Hill (Boers defeated)	,, 20, 1899
Glencoe, or Dundee (Boers defeated)	,, 20, 1899
Elandslaagte (Boers defeated)	,, 21, 1899
Mafeking Bombarded (Boers repulsed)	,, 23, 1899
Nicholsons Nek (British defeated)	,, 30, 1899
Belmont (Boers defeated)	Nov.23, 1899
Enslin or Graspan (Boers defeated)	,, 25, 1899
Modder River (Methuen forces Cronje	

to quit his position)	,, 28,	1900
Spion Kop (captured by the British and afterwards evacuated)	,, 17–24,	1900
Relief of Kimberley	Feb. 15,	1900
Relief of Ladysmith	,, 28,	1900
Relief of Mafeking	May 17–18,	1900
General Botha captured	,, 29,	1900
Philip Botha killed at Doomberg	March	1901
Death of Mr. Cecil Rhodes	,, 6,	1902
Signing of Peace	May 31,	1902

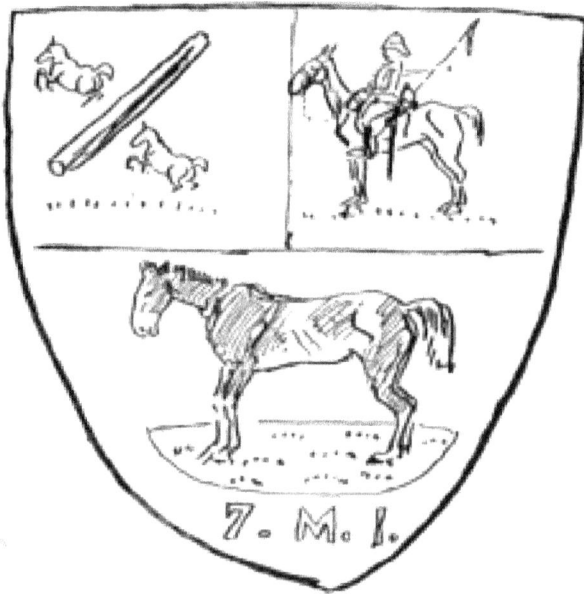

This is the 7th Mounted Infantry crest; any member of the Royal College of Heraldry will read it as follows:

Cavalry with a bar sinister, rampant on a field *vert* a sore-backed Argent(ine).

CHAPTER 1

From Ireland to the Cape

It was about the beginning of December when at last we got orders and were for the front after all. For weeks I had watched the transports steaming out between Forts Carlisle and Camden, in the latter of which my company was on detachment; and had even seen the *Simla* take out the plum puddings for the first Christmas of the war, before we were relieved by the Stafford Militia, rejoined the regiment at Cork and were embarked on one of those horrors of the soldier returning from or going on furlough—a Cork-Milford pig-boat.

I will draw a veil over that awful crossing, and take up the thread at Milford Station.

Here I had the luck to be told off as one of the corporals of the colour party, so that I rode in a first-class carriage, with a colour-sergeant, another corporal, and the colours.

The journey to Aldershot was a triumph; all England was mad over the war, and a soldier was worth what he could drink in any company in the kingdom. We got an ovation at every station, and were adjured by people who probably didn't know whether the incident they referred to occurred in the Mutiny or Crimea, to "remember Majuba Hill."

After having remembered it a sufficiency of times we arrived at Aldershot and took up some barracks (whether Albuera, Salamanca, Alma, or what, I cannot now remember; but it was in Stanhope Lines, I think—anyway, it does not matter). Here we spent Christmas, and were pretty comfortable till the reserves arrived. These men were the popular heroes at the time, and undoubtedly were indispensable then, and formed the backbone of the army in South Africa; but—they put fifteen years on every non-commissioned officer in the service doing duty at the time they "came up." I was "orderly sergeant for the ensuing week," and I know!

I didn't see much of England in the war-fever, as I was always answering for other N.C.O.'s who had relatives near and were on pass to visit them, so rarely left barracks; and I was most heartily glad when we entrained for Southampton and embarked amidst "great enthusiasm" (most of the regiment came from Southampton and Portsmouth) on the P. & O. boat *Assaya*, a brand-new boat and well found. We lived as well on her as in barracks. I suppose I ought to know who saw us off and what speeches were made, etc., but I was too much interested in the doings of some of the aforementioned convivial reservists, who were having a good time on the quay with their friends and admirers, and seeing no reason why they should cut it short, would not do so until persuaded by a corporal and file.

The voyage was uneventful, nothing much being done beside the hour's physical drill, bar concerts in the evening, and gambling[1] all day. The only place we touched at was Las Palmas, which is much like Brindisi or any of the Mediterranean ports to look at—rather prettier perhaps—but of course we were not allowed on shore. It seems queer now, but the principal idea amongst us then and for some time after we landed, was that we should be too late, and that peace would be declared before we had fired a shot. That was in the first January of the war!

Cape Town was rather a disappointment, the Table Mountain not coming up to one's expectations. We drew close up to the quay—in fact our train that was to take us up to the front was right alongside the boat. I am afraid the thing that impressed me

1. Some energetic chap at home has just discovered that gambling goes on in troopships, and is getting up an inquiry about it. Gambling always has been winked at on troopships as the best way of keeping the men amused. Our Chaplain used to watch, and I have seen him stake money till he lost, with the object of showing the men that it was possible to lose without using foul language about it.

most was the fruit—a helmet full of glorious grapes for three-pence. Certain loyal inhabitants did wonders in the way of a welcome for us; the station was hung with welcoming standards, there were free refreshment stands, and when we were finally entrained children and ladies came along with great baskets of fruit which they distributed; in fact, it was a repetition of the Milford to Aldershot excursion.

Our regimental badges were in great request here, a tiger from our caps fetching a sovereign, or at the least a bottle of whiskey. (With my usual neglect of business opportunities I had given all my badges, roses, laurels, tigers, and all to the first little girl that asked me for them.)

We wasted very little time before we started, our immediate destination being De Aar, which, as far as I recollect, is a dust-heap two or three stations south of Orange River. It took us, I think, four days training through at first Indian-like scenery, then rocky *kloofs* and defiles, and finally sandy *karroo*, the line being defended right down to Cape Town by the Duke of Edinburgh's Volunteer Rifles, a colonial corps. We got pretty good receptions at all the stations, some of them pretty little green places; but one could not help noticing people here and there of a cast of countenance with which one was not familiar, who held aloof from the crowd and regarded us without much enthusiasm-Cape Dutch, evidently.

We only spent one night in De Aar (enough, however, to fill us up with sand), and next day trained down to Orange River in coal trucks. Here the 7th Division was forming up, and we joined the Norfolks (they had come out with us in the *Assaya*), Lincolns, K.O.S.B.'s, and the remainder of the Brigade. Our Mounted Infantry company under Major Welch (which I had been trying to join un- successfully) left us here to form a company of the 7th Mounted Infantry

After a couple of days or so, I got my first taste of marching under an African sun—although the remainder went by train, for some reason the Hants marched to Enslin. Three days, if I re-member right, it took us, and the heat and thirst was pretty bad after three weeks on the ship; however, we turned up smiling, having marched over the battlefields of Belmont and Graspan, where we found the dead horses very much in evidence. We camped alongside the line, and remained there for two or three days; we were pretty glad of the rest and chance of changing clothes and cleaning up a bit. Meanwhile, I'll explain the situation as far as I knew it myself.

Ladysmith and Mafeking, of course, were still unrelieved, Buller being stuck at the Tugela, and Gatacre down Stormberg way. Methuen was some fifteen miles ahead of us on the Modder, with Cronje on the other side of the fence; we could see the helio in daytime and the searchlight at night from Kimberley, over the heads of the two. So things were at a deadlock, and yet so utterly ignorant were the rank and file (I won't answer for the officers) that none of us believed the affair would last six months at the most! We saw several small batches of prisoners, who also were rather disappointing,[2] being much like old Whitman or any old English farmer or small tradesmen—some, indeed, very like old Jimmy Whitman and Methuen's hospital trains were passing all day for Cape Town and the base hospitals.

So matters stood when one day we got orders to hold ourselves in readiness for a night march. Where we were going we did not know, as usual; we certainly did not care much, so long as a move of some sort was on. Roberts we knew was in charge of us, and French had just come round from the other side (Ladysmith or somewhere) to take over all the cavalry. We were told to leave our camps standing, as we were only going out for a few days (we got used to that little joke afterwards), and that night we fell in with a rolled blanket, 200 rounds of ammunition, and three days' bully beef and biscuit. We only just crossed the line towards the Free State, and then lay down in the ranks, under a glorious starry African night, while the Division formed up. If we had known it, we were not to get a night's rest, hardly a proper halt, till Bloemfontein!

---

2. These, I think, must have been local men from stores, etc., on the line, being very different from the High Veldt and Magaliesberg Boers of Cronje's command.

CHAPTER 2

The Start

It got pretty cold towards morning, lying there in thin khaki with nothing over you, and I don't think anyone was sorry when, about 2 a.m., the word was passed (no bugle-calls were allowed) to fall in; and we rose up stiff with cold, and remained in the ranks while regiment after regiment, and battery after battery, filed past to their places in the scheme. At last our turn came, and we moved off in the grey, cold, miserable sort of morning twilight, over a small stony *kopje*, and then across a scrubby plain crossed at regular intervals by stone ridges the low Free State *kopjes* that we were to have so much experience of later.

Due east we went towards Koffyfontein, and camped that night after an uneventful and fairly easy march at Ramdam,

which is a farm with a big dam and fine fruit garden. I just had time to have a feed of fruit (beautiful grapes, figs, and peaches) when my company was told off for outpost duty, and we got out just before dusk and took up a position on one of the above-mentioned *kopjes*. I was in charge of one post of three men-the corporal's duty is to post the sentries and see they do their sentry-go properly; he has to change reliefs every two hours, and he doesn't get much sleep.

There was a large Boer force[1] at Jacobsdal, which is not very far as the crow flies from Ramdam, so we were pretty wide awake, as it was the first time we had done outpost with nothing between us and the enemy.

We were well in the Free State now, and were, I believe, the first force of any size to invade it, so we had the sense that at last we were doing something definite. I slept for a short time under the skyline, on the uncommonly stony side of the *kop*, and was awakened about an hour before dawn by a dull sort of roar like waves on a shingly beach; this was French moving out with his mounted troops and artillery.

From then till long after daylight I watched them, and it was one of the finest sights I've ever seen. First, regiment after regiment of cavalry and Mounted Infantry came up to the foot of the *kopje* I was on, in column of troops, looking at a distance, in the half light, like a smudge on the dark grey of the *veldt*; then, as they got nearer the light caught some parts of their equipment, and gradually showed them up—some thousands of mounted men, silent except for the horses' hoofs and now and then a stumble or the rattle of a carbine-bucket.

As they reached the foot of my *kopje*, each troop in turn got the order "Sub-sections, left!" and they wheeled in fours and filed through a road that was cut through the rocks, and opened out again the other side. Then came the guns—I don't know how many, but it seemed as if there was no end to them—and it was wonderful the way they worked them over that *kopje*. There was not time for them all to file through the road, so they just

---

1. De Wet.

16

came straight at it and over, driving over stones as big as chairs.

The fires were all lighted in our camp long before dawn, and our breakfast, or rather, the day's ration of coffee (we had biscuits and bully with us), was sent out; and just about as the last of French's guns cleared the *kopje*, the head of our column started out, and we fell in as the regiment passed, and started the second day's march.

If the first day had given us the idea that we were going to have an easy job the second made up for it, want of water being the chief trouble. We had had it pretty rough on the march from Orange River to Enslin, but this was worse; we only struck one well all day, and of course all the column could not get water, as it had to be drawn, and we only waited about an hour. For my part I had no drink at all, all day, except the pint or so of coffee in the morning, and to us, unaccustomed as we were to the climate, a twenty-mile march over *veldt* with no water was no joke. I was jolly glad, then and all through the war, that I was thin, as I saw the big, fat men naturally suffered more from heat, etc.

We had heard the guns nearly all day in front of us: that was the mounted troops, and they had a few casualties, I believe, an officer of the Rifles being killed; but we didn't get into the fighting, and camped that night at a farm on the Piet River, near Koffyfontein, where there were a lot of sheep. We stayed there all next day, having a good blow-out of mutton and a sleep, both of which were very welcome; but about 7 p.m. that night we fell in hurriedly, and trekked off almost the way we had come; none of us knew where we were going, but we had a hazy idea that something was wrong. Well, we trekked all that night hard and nearly all next day, and night marching on foot over the *veldt* is no joke at all. (If you are not falling into ant-bear holes you are tumbling over ant-heaps.)

We halted about five miles from Jacobsdal and thought we were going to have a rest, but had only just piled arms and lay down, too done up to swear, when we were roused out again about 5 p.m., and marched off in a new direction. Men were falling out by now, but we kept on till 10 or 11 p.m., when we halted on a grassy slope and lay down. I heard two or three guns go off somewhere, and then I went to sleep till we moved off again just before daybreak—pretty cold, too—back to the camp near Jacobsdal. I subsequently learnt that we had been out to try and save the convoy that De Wet got, but the oxen were gone, so we had to abandon it—burning it first, though,[2] which accounted for some of the troops having all sorts of stores of cocoa and luxuries of sorts for the next day or two. If I hadn't gone to sleep I might have—but no matter, I had a sleep, and provisions had not assumed such an aspect of vast importance as they did in a day or two. We found our company of Mounted Infantry here, and I went and had an envious look at their horses. We slept there that night, and next morning marched to Jacobsdal, which had been taken the day before.

We arrived about 11 a.m. and pitched camp—evidently we were going to get a few minutes halt here—had dinner, took our boots off (first time since Enslin) and putties, and had a most luxurious siesta all the afternoon—began to think contemptuously of marching—had tea about 4 p.m. (jam for tea!), and were thinking of turning in (even thought of half undressing), when whistles sounded for orderly-sergeants, and presently it was given out: "Pack up at once; the Division moves at 6"!! Well, the curses were so fervid as to be almost tearful, but there was no help for it; French was supposed to be in trouble somewhere ahead (and we knew it was a long way, as we could see a good deal farther than we felt inclined to walk), and we were to go and back him up.

I am afraid we were not so enthusiastic in those days as we might have been about French's rapid movements, as we always had to try to keep somewhere in call behind him,

We marched all that night, halted for an hour in the morning for a drink of coffee, and marched again all the day. About noon we could hear big guns in front and plenty of them; and I was beginning to pray for a shell to hit me by way of getting

---

2. De Wet in his book says he got all the convoy away, so there must have been some wagons he had not enough cattle for.

a rest, when we rounded a *kopje* about 6 p.m., and marched out on a sort of plateau overlooking the Modder River, and at last halted. We had left our wagons miles behind, so just piled arms and lay down and went to sleep till about midnight, when the cold woke me. After that I walked about (or rather, hobbled; my feet were pretty sore and stiff) for ten minutes, then slept as long as the cold would let me, till dawn.

As I could see no prospect of breakfast, and the regiment didn't appear to be taking much interest in things, I followed a lot who were going down to the river for a drink. It was chiefly by luck that we struck our own men down there, for we didn't know that Cronje and his men were *laager*ed up in the riverbed. However, we found the Gordons' camp just in time to see four wagon-loads of dead brought in who had been killed in yesterday's fighting. Most of them were hit in the kilt—that was before the khaki apron was worn by the Jocks.

When I got back to the battalion, the wagons were just arriving; so I had a couple of biscuits and some bully, and for the rest of that day we watched the troops down the river shelling Cronje's *laager* (we didn't know it was Cronje then). Then, in the evening, the battalion was split up into companies, and we all had different posts assigned to us; this, of course, was forming the ring round the *laager*. We were not sure what we were going to do, but from the decided and rather bustling way things were done we judged that something was up; anyway, there evidently was not another night march (we thought), and we didn't worry about much else.

My company was posted on a small and uncommonly rocky *kopje*. I think from a later visit to the place that it must have been just opposite the Paardeberg Drift.[3] We had hardly got told off to our posts when we were called down the *kopje*; and after hanging about in the dusty road till about 11 p.m., we were marched off three or four miles, I should think, and took up a position on another drift. I did not know why at the time, but it must have been that they heard about De Wet coming to try

3. On the other side of the river from Paardeberg Kop.

and relieve Cronje.

We stayed there all night and next day, in a dry, sandy water-course, but as soon as it was dark off we went back again—past Lord Roberts's position at Paardeberg Drift, past the *laager* (we could see the lights in it, and we were so close that we were ordered not to talk), and on to another drift, where we waited till morning, when we crossed the river, wading through up to our breasts. There was the grave of a man of the Essex Regiment, just where we crossed; we knew his regiment by the helmet which was laid at the head.

We were now on the same side of the river as Cronje, and we marched towards the *laager* from the side furthest from where Lord Roberts was at the Paardeberg Kop. Very cautiously we went the last half mile, till we struck the Essex, who were in the dry gullies in the river bank within rifle shot of the *laager*. They promptly cleared out the way we had come, and we were left to our own devices. Each company took possession of a dry *mullah*, and proceeded with the business we were there for, namely, making trenches leading in a zig-zag way towards the *laager*.

We spent an awful week here on account of the rainy nights. Our routine was as follows: gangs of so many men, whole companies at a time, working in the trenches—I forget how the reliefs went, but I know we hardly got any sleep, and just a few minutes for meals. Of course, we were under fire always in the trenches, but that was a small matter, as we always had good cover—not much worse than marking in the butts at home, except now and then when one had to go with a message or something over exposed ground, when it was pretty warm.

But the nights when we were off duty were the worst, as we had absolutely no shelter, and it rained regularly and heavily every blessed night. You would look for a level-looking place in your particular ditch about sundown, put on your big coat, wrap a blanket round you, and lie down—so far, good! But in the dark of the night you'd wake with an ominous rumbling in the air, of thunder, and soon after that, plop-plop!—a few drops as big as half-crowns, and then down it comes. Not much good moving,

PAARDEBERG

A Paardeberg Kop from which Lord Roberts probably directed affairs.
B Conical kopje opposite Paardeberg Drift.
C Position of hospital, also other side of drift.
D Ridge from which bag guns fired on laager.
E Position of Highland Brigade (after first day).
F Ground over which the fighting took place first day (Canadian charge, etc.).
G Cronje's laager.
H Position of Hants in trenches.
J Position of Norfolks in trenches.
X X French's guns.
K French's probable camp.
L Koodoos-Rand Drift.
M Poplar Grove.
N Direction of Kimberley.
O Road to Modder River station, along which Cronje had trekked probably; there was another road behind the kopje P.

but you get as far on the slant of the bank as you can so as not to lie in more of a puddle than you can help, pull your blanket well over your head and stick it, and the water runs down the bank in rivulets.

You probably go to sleep all right, but waking in the morning is pure joy—your big coat has kept the top half of you fairly dry, but the side you lie on, and your feet and legs up to your knees are sure to be wet through, and you wrap your soaking blanket round your shoulders and sit on a sloppy bank with a miserable, cold wind blowing through you. Then you squelch your toes in your boots and think of barrack-room beds, hammocks on a dry troop deck, or any other dry and warm place where one can get a comfortable sleep; and if you don't curse the Boers and British and everyone who had any hand in the war, it's because you haven't enough vitality left.

Then just as it's beginning to turn a bit grey in the east (which in any circumstances is the most miserable time of the twenty-four hours), you've got to turn out and go and do something, when every movement presses some part of sodden clothing— very cold—up against your skin, and little tricklets of cold water run down till they collect in your putties, where they soak.

Soon, at sunrise, the bullets start whistling through the bushes; and now and then there's a bang, and a shell comes along, sounding as if it was tearing all the trees in sight up by the roots,

till it bursts against the opposite bank. When you think of the hospital train with plenty of food and a blanket (even if it is lousy) in a dry marquee, you're not sure that you wouldn't like to be hit yourself!

Once the sun is up, however, everything is all right (bar short rations), for it soon dries you through, and if you had enough to eat you might almost fancy you were having a picnic, as it is a pretty place, with willow trees and trees like the *divvy-divvy* in India right down to the water's edge, and any amount of doves and birds like the mina making a tremendous row all day.

So things went on for a week or two, Cronje lying low and saying nothing, and our guns dumping shells into him all day. There were very few casualties on our side after the first few days, when the Canadians' bayonet charge, etc., happened: they are history, so I needn't describe them. I did not see it myself. I heard afterwards that our Mounted Infantry company which, you remember, we last saw at Jacobsdal, being among the first up, advanced with much confidence (they were about sixty strong) against the *laager*, like a fox-terrier pup interfering with a mastiff with a bone, and with much the same result. They left several wounded, when they remembered an appointment somewhere else, and these were taken into the *laager* and well treated till the surrender.

The Boers seemed to get very jumpy the last two or three nights of the siege; they could see the trenches getting close up, and they were always mortally afraid of the bayonet. (With reason, too, as they were only armed for long-range fighting, and several had been bayoneted the first day or two—they were up in trees, and let our men pass and then sniped them from behind. Naturally Tommy was annoyed, so when they discovered the game they shook the trees and caught Brother Boer on the point when he jumped; if he didn't jump, he was potted, poor devil! Captain Richards of ours shot one in a tree like this.)

As I was saying, the last night or so heavy firing was kept up from the *laager*, and at daybreak on Majuba day a crowd of white flags went up. I didn't see Cronje; but the *laager* was in an awful

23

state: dead horses and cattle and half buried dead men; the stink was fearful. There were a lot of women there: they had come down to keep Majuba day on commando. Of course, they were in shell-proof places in the river bank. After the prisoners had been packed off, we all moved over to a farm called Osfontein, where we camped for a few days still on about quarter rations and pretty heavy outpost duty, as De Wet was hanging round our front.

That night was one of the wettest I've had. We had put up blanket bivouacs (just two blankets slung over a string and inhabited by three men) and everyone in camp was turned in, being pretty done up. About 9 p.m. a real South African thunderstorm came on. The lightning stampeded the horses, and they were galloping about the camp over bivouacs or anywhere (one trod on a man's face!); and the rain came down like pouring out tea. Of course blanket bivouacs are no use for heavy rain; most of them (mine for one) were beaten flat in five minutes, and in ten the whole camp was ankle deep, and it still rained. My chum and I crawled out and surveyed the landscape not a dry spot in Africa apparently; so we waded to the edge of the camp, and got up in a thorn tree (we had our big coats on); and we sat in that bally old tree in a steady, cold rain from 9 p.m. till reveille!

BLANKET BIVOUACS

CHAPTER 3

Early Experiences

After a day or so we marched along the river some five miles (they couldn't get more a day out of us, we were so starved down). I was out on the left flank with a few men—I don't know why, as there were troops all round us—and I came across the sergeant-major of our Mounted Infantry company. He had been rather a pal of mine at home (it was that Sergeant Weston that I wrote to the time I got the extension of furlough, and Dad was so horrified at my addressing him as "Jack," when I was only a lance-corporal; he was killed afterwards at Onverwacht), and I told him to try all he knew to get me on the Mounted Infantry, as I was about full of the infantry. He said he would, and kept

IN A THORN TREE

his word.

The next thing of importance was Poplar Grove. We were warned overnight that there was a big thing coming off next day, and packed up camp ready, sleeping in the ranks practically. Some time before daylight (which is a most depressing time to look forward to an engagement, especially on an empty stomach) we fell in and trekked towards some low *kopjes*, coming up at right angles to the river.

For some reason all the field officers were on foot, and as I was left guide of No. 1 (A Company), poor old Colonel Briggs was walking alongside me; he was not used to walking and felt the heat, frequently telling me to give a shorter step! Our formation as we approached the *kop* was column of regiments, each regiment extending in a long single rank from the river on the left to some low hills on the right, ours being about the fifth regiment.

Presently the Boers opened with two guns from the *kopje* in front, and gave each regiment as they reached a certain spot three or four shells (it was a common practice with the Boers to get the range of a certain object and hammer anything that came near it). Every shell burst a few paces in front of the right-hand companies as they came up, till the K.O.S.B.'s, I think it was, who were next in front of us, and they got one shell fair in the ranks, I believe killing four men. You can imagine my relief at this juncture to hear the order:

"A Company move to the right in file, right turn!" and we were moved off to the right, then "left wheel!" and we went on as a right flank guard, and missed the marked place. Presently, however, the firing stopped; and when we marched over the spur of the hill we found the Boer position deserted—tents left standing, blankets and kit lying all over the place—evidently it had been a panic; I got some German rusks out of a tent, which were a godsend.

After this we formed up in quarter columns and marched down to the river to camp. It was now that Colonel Briggs walked beside me; he remarked that it had been a bloodless victory, in which I heartily concurred, as I did not know for days after that that was all there was of the "battle" of Poplar Grove). We know now that French's cavalry had gone round and threatened their retreat, and the war as a general rule has proved that, to make a good stand, the Boer must know that he can get away if he likes, which is curious when you come to think of it.

Our regiment was left here for three days waiting for a convoy, so missed Driefontein. We camped at a farm which had been hit by a shell that day; there was a Boer inside who had been hit by the same shell! We had a jolly camp here all among the trees, but precious little to help out the picnic idea in the way of eatables. Even when the convoy came we were still on half rations,[1] and he was a lucky man who could steal a handful of *mealies* (the maize that you feed fowls on at home) from the wagon mules. You boiled these *mealies* and mashed them, and they were filling if nothing else. We took the convoy on after the others towards Petursberg, finding them the second day.

One incident near Petursberg I must mention, if only in defence of the much abused Rooinek ("khaki" now he is known as). We camped on a plain near a good farmhouse, and soon after I went down to the farm for water. There were two women and several girls there, and for a wonder no officers, staff or otherwise, at the house. There was a crowd of men from every branch of the column, and the women seemed to be in difficulties, there was such a crowd. Seeing I was a corporal, one of them asked me to keep them quiet and she would sell them stuff.

So I fell them in, and each man was served in his turn till she couldn't spare any more, when they dispersed quietly. I doubt if in any army of the Continent one corporal could keep order among men from every regiment of a column, in an enemy's farmyard, with plenty of fowls, etc., running about—half-starved men, too, and they had to pay a good price. I must admit a doubt as to whether it could have been done later in the war among the mounted troops; but it was their business to clear the farms,

---

1. We wore the letters H.R. in our helmets, for Hants Regiment, but when asked we used to say it stood for "Half Rations."

so the question does not arise. The woman, who said she was the wife of a commandant, was so pleased that she gave me a good feed (without any "moral suasion").

There was a good deal of sickness amongst us at this time, owing probably to the bad water at Paardeberg (we had to drink from the river in which the Boers had thrown dead horses, cattle, and even men), and I think I had a narrow escape. Though I say it myself, I had never in my soldiering fallen out on a march, either at home (where the manoeuvres are no joke) or out here in the marching I have already mentioned; but about two days before Bloemfontein I began to feel queer in the afternoon[2] on the march. The regiment was either out on the flank or rear-guard, as no one seemed to be behind, bar the mounted screen.

Well, I got worse and worse, till at last I couldn't keep up at all, so asked leave from my company officer (Mr. Ashby; he was very sick, too, with dysentery!) to fall out. In order to fall out you got a ticket signed by your officer, and this entitled you to ride on any conveyance you could climb on to (they were pretty chary with these tickets, too, I've heard, though I only wanted one once, so don't know). Well, my ticket was not much use to me, as I should have had to run to catch anything on wheels, and I couldn't have run a yard to save my life, so I kept dropping behind further and further, till the mounted troops had passed me and it got dark; and there I was, feeling as if the sooner I died the better I should like it.

"I FALL OUT"

2. And in the inside.

28

Most romantic situation, now I think of it, don't you know!-wild moonlight *veldt*, slow music, and a dying soldier writing his last letter. It didn't strike me so at the time, though; in fact, I never felt less romantic in my life. I was just thinking of camping down for the night when I saw lights ahead where they were camped, and crawled into camp and flopped down without troubling to draw a blanket or anything, fully intending to die in the night (or at least directly after breakfast in the morning). In the morning, to my astonishment, I was all right, and never felt any more of it! Most disappointing, after I had forgiven all my enemies and got myself into a most Christian state of mind.

Nothing of any importance happened now till we got to a place where there are two big dams close together about eight or nine miles out of Bloemfontein, and here our brigade camped down, and we were able to get a ripping bath and rest. Food also became a little less of a rarity, as they could get a little out from Bloemfontein, which had surrendered without a shot being fired. Next day, I and the man who had spent the night in the tree with me (Harvey was his name, a lance-corporal) were seized with a consuming desire to see a civilised town and have a good feed; so we put in a pass and tramped off to Bloemfontein.

Eight miles was nothing to us, of course; so we arrived pretty fit and very hungry. Bloemfontein wore rather a dismal appearance, all the public places being closed, and most of the stores sold out—everything at famine prices. However, we discovered a place where you could get a feed at a fixed rate—5s. or something—and sat down and ordered ham and eggs. You don't know the full possibilities of ham and eggs until you've been some months on dog biscuit, and precious little of that.

We were the first discoverers of this little place apparently, as no one else was in; and we sat down to a nice little table where they had promiscuously placed loaves of bread, pats of butter and jugs of milk (just imagine it!). We finished everything on the table and called for more before the ham and eggs were cooked, and altogether ate about 16s. worth each, I should say. I never

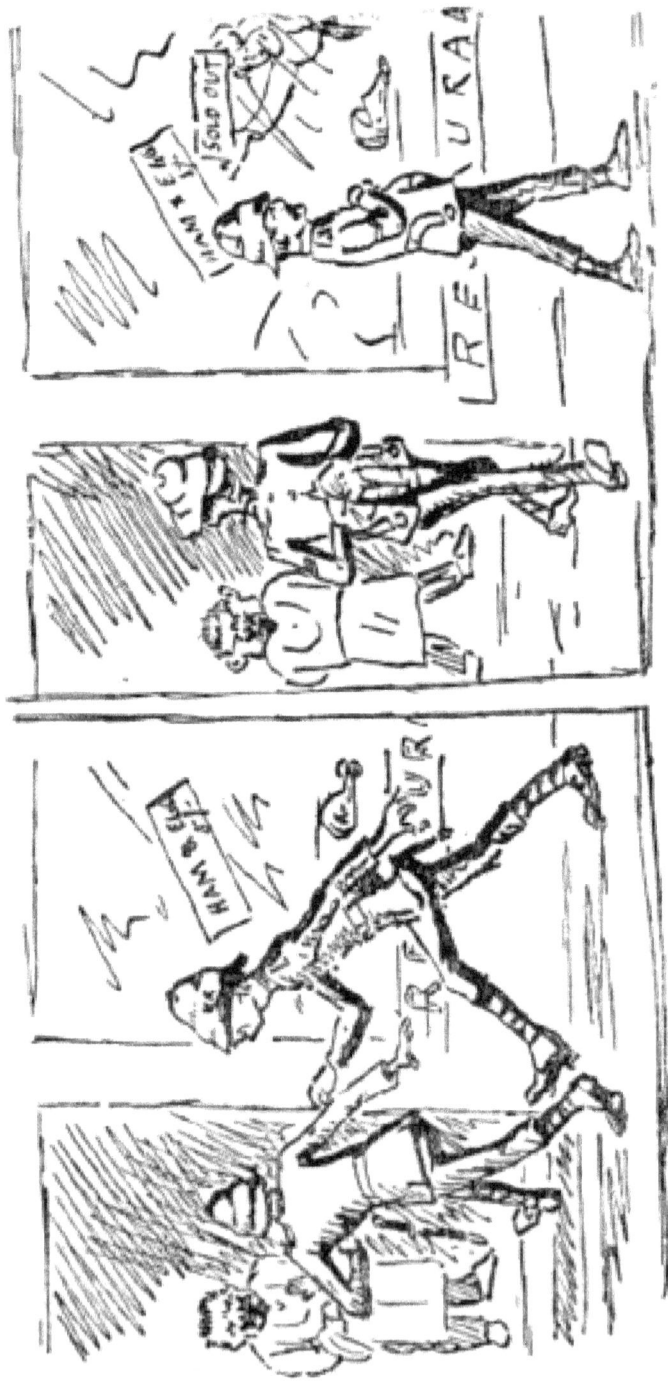

Ham and eggs at Bloemfontein

had such a glorious feed in my life; we could hardly walk about the town afterwards. We went back there for tea, but they saw us coming, and put up their prices about threefold.

Bloemfontein in ordinary times must be a very pretty little place—a lot of trees, and every house with a pretty garden. The name means "fountain of flowers," and the buildings are pretty—dazzling white and red roofs and green painted woodwork. On the way out we struck our Mounted Infantry company just outside the town, and had a chat with them. The sergeant-major told me that they were going to apply for some more men from the battalion, so I was to look out and put in my name as soon as it came out, and he would speak to Major Welch about me.

I had a lot of old friends in the Mounted Infantry company, so went down the horse lines and was talking to them till nearly dark. They had already started on their career of crime as horse-stealers, and offered to lift a horse for each of us to ride home on, if we would return the saddle and bridle! (It didn't matter about the horse.) But not being accustomed to that sort of thing (then) I declined, at which they were rather offended.

We remained at Quaggafontein (the name of the two-dam place) two or three days, and the band-master (acting), being of a speculative turn of mind, made a small fortune by borrowing a commando wagon and toting out loads of flour from Bloemfontein, which he sold at 1s. the canteen full. We used to have great feeds with this, making *jupatties* and all sorts of messes.

There was no wood near camp, so we used to burn the roots of a sort of scrub not much bigger than a cabbage; and it was very funny to see groups of two or three men, scattered all over camp in the evenings, over little two-candle-power fires, "cooking"! The aforementioned Harvey was my confederate in all these affairs. There were four of us in mess, but we two were the only ones who took any interest in things, as of the other two corporals one was nearly dead with dysentery and the other of starvation and marching, and they did nothing but lie in the bivouac and sleep.

After a day or two we moved camp close to Bloemfontein,

and all the divisions and brigades were got together in order again. Next day Lord Roberts reviewed us, and then he published general orders.

The first order was a sort of summary of what we had done in the month—how we had put an entirely different aspect on the war by capturing Cronje, etc.; that our march from Jacobsdal to Paardeberg was one of the finest feats of modern warfare, in the circumstances being ahead of the Kandahar march, etc.; in fact, we took a lot of beating one way and another, and he had no doubt we would keep it up.

Number 2 was to the effect that if any of us blackguards were caught looting so much as a hen's egg from any private person—Dutch, English, or Kaffir—we would be tried by drumhead court-martial and instantly shot!! I took a copy of that lot of orders as a memento, but it was lost, with the only diary I ever have kept or will keep again, during certain strategic moments which I will detail later. (It is not a fact that I threw my coat and other impedimenta away to lighten my horse during one of those "Tod Sloan "affairs that Kipling refers to.)

Then at last it came out that men were wanted for the Mounted Infantry, and I put in for it at once. My company officer offered no objection; he even seemed rather pleased at the thought of parting with me! He was on special service from India—a most energetic man; I had not had much to do with him, but we didn't hit it much.

Major Welch rode over and gave me instructions—I was the senior corporal of the party going on the Mounted Infantry; there was another corporal and about thirty men—and that afternoon I marched the party off through Bloemfontein to the Mounted Infantry camp at Rustfontein, and was a mounted man at last.

We had about three days of extemporised riding school (I could ride quite well enough for the Mounted Infantry before, thanks to the old grey jumping pony) and then went to duty. I was *serre-file* to No. 1 section, and got a ripping little black horse. By his hoof marks he was a Bengal Lancer, and I kept him about ten months, which is a good record for the trekking we did: three months generally killed them.

CHAPTER 4

"Mounted Infantry"

For the month that Lord Roberts lay in Bloemfontein to recruit, my company (of M.I) was on the outpost line at Fischer's farm (the delegate to America), a beautiful place with tennis courts and lovely gardens—deserted, though! We had a pretty good time here, and food was actually obtainable: we even got bread rations, and as there were any amount of spring-buck about we did not go short of meat.

We could see scattered parties of Boers moving about in the direction of the Modder, but they left us alone, though we had several night alarms. Practically the only duty we did was Cossack posts—a corporal and six men posted for a day and night on a knoll about two miles from camp. As there were plenty of Kaffir *kraals* about, these posts used to live pretty well! We had been here nearly a month when I was told off to take charge of a funeral party to bury a man who had died in Bloemfontein.

While I was at the hospital waiting, I heard the account of Sanna's Post (which had just taken place) from some of the wounded. I guessed that something would have to be done on our side, and was not surprised when a few days later, while I was on Cossack post, I got an order to come in at once. We went in at the canter, and found the camp struck and everything ready to move off.

As soon as I reported we trekked off, reaching Bloemfontein about dark, and joined a large mounted force (Ian Hamilton's Mounted Infantry), and moved on at once towards Thaba'nchu, marching till about 1 a.m., when we lay down with the reins over our arms till daylight, and then went on to the waterworks. Several men had been left behind at Fischer's farm, without horses, with some Australians, who were in charge of sick horses.

These Australians were good men, but they used to rather fancy themselves as knowing sort of cards—especially where stock was concerned—so that it rather amused us when some of the men we had left rolled up next morning mounted on jolly good Australian whalers, and with full Australian outfits! This march, by the way, was another three days' joke, as we had been told we were going for a four days' reconnaissance; this time we brought up at Pretoria. Well, when we got to Sanna's Post it was quite a typical battlefield—dead horses, wheels of guns and wagons, helmets, bayonets, etc., all over the place, and we reburied several bodies that had been partially washed out by the heavy rains that had fallen.

As we approached the waterworks we opened out a bit, as the enemy was known to be in the hills the other side of the river; and just as we got down to the buildings they opened with two 15-pounders, and made it pretty warm for a bit. One company went down and took possession of the waterworks buildings, and the rest of us retired to the half-built station (they were making a line out to Ladybrand) and camped down.

Next morning we were up early (in fact we always started before sun-up: you'd be awakened at what you thought was midnight by the sentries on the horse lines chopping wood for their particular mess's fire). We got through the hills on the Modder without a shot being fired, and then the Mounted Infantry went off ahead. It was a grand feeling to me riding a good, lively little horse past the foot-sloggers, one of whom I had been myself on my last trek.

About half-way between the waterworks and Thaba'nchu we struck them in some very rough *kopje*, and the 7th Mounted Infantry went off to the left to get round their flank. They were firing on us at long ranges, for two or three miles; but we got round without getting to close quarters, and camped under a

Bloemfontein.   Beachman's Kop.   Sanna's Post.

WATERWORKS

high *kopje*, which I had to climb as lookout post. We found the little *schanges* the Boers had built and their empty cartridge cases, and could see them clearing in the distance like flies running over a billiard table.

Next day we went into Thaba'nchu, with very little fighting; and my company was on a *spitz kop* (conical *kopje*), with a Kaffir *kraal* at the foot; so we lived on fowl and eggs. We stayed at Thaba'nchu for a few days, going out for a row every day the Boers were in the hills behind the town, Ladybrand way. I got my first experience of a pom-pom here—we were lying out on a ridge, sniping the foes in front very comfortably, when a little beast of a pom-pom sneaked up on our flank to a *nek* about 500 yards away, and proceeded to make things hum. We heard "pom-pom-pom" about seven or eight times, like a side drum giving the step at spring drills—only faster. We didn't know what it meant, so took no notice—till there was a screech like an engine letting off steam, and then bang-bang-bang at precisely the same intervals as the first, and they were spitting and bursting right between us and our horses which were about twenty yards away. We left!

Then, one morning when we were camped (still at Thaba'nchu) right under the mountain, they got two big guns—Creusots, I should think—right on top of another mountain about six miles off; and just as we were getting the coffee boiled at dawn, they lobbed two shells right into camp just behind our rear horse-lines. I saw, in the confusion, two men of one of our other companies carried off on stretchers; but we had to pick up everything and track off round a spur of the hill where they couldn't see us.

Of course, we heard the shells coming, but we felt so secure in our position that we hardly realised that they were shells till they burst. At that distance you don't hear the report of the gun till after the whistle of the shell! You may be sitting quite comfortably, drinking coffee or anything, and first you are conscious of a sort of vibration like you hear on a line when a train is a long way off, which turns to a sort of screech as it goes over (if it goes over), and dies away again, till it hits "whomp"! If it's shrapnel, of course it cuts off in the middle of a screech, with a hair-raising bang; and then you hear the bullets thumping all round you. Shrapnel was my pet aversion!

Next move we made we were rushed off about eight miles to the southward. De Villiers or someone was coming up from Smithfield way, and we had to hold a post (which is a pass—in this case between two mountains almost as high as Thaba'nchu itself). We shinned up the one to the left, and immediately got recalled, so went down again. This was a mistake, as directly we got to our horses we were ordered up again, which improved our muscles if not our tempers.

I was about done when we got to the top, so it was not an unmixed evil that as soon as we showed on the top we had to lie as flat as a pancake and stay there for about two hours, without so much as kneeling up, while some sporting Boers on the next ridge were trying to see how near they could get without hitting us; in fact, one or two were careless and cut it too fine, judging by the language of one Tommy who was helped down the hill close to me with one more hole in his pants.

It was pretty warm as they got a cross-fire in, which prevented us from having our share of the shooting. We saw a big column coming from the expected direction, but it turned out to be a cavalry brigade; so we went home after our friends had got tired and had gone.

COVER

38

All this time our horses were getting more than they could eat, as they were on full rations, besides what we could pick up in the shape of *mealies* and oat-hay—they were up to the knees in the latter every night, for this is the best part of the Free State, and they had had an exceptionally good year. The result was the horses were up to any amount of work and as fresh as paint-and at that time we got horses, not cab-horses broken down.

There was many an exciting event brought off out on the flanks, when a convenient ridge hid you from the company, between men away on flank guard (two of them fancied their mounts a bit), and some pretty tall betting, too. I, as lance-corporal, ought to have stopped these, but then I had the fastest horse!! So what could I do? The reason, I think, that my mount kept his condition longest was that he was a kicker, and after he had lamed several on the horse line I got orders to peg him out by himself, which I did with a long rope, so he could graze all night while the others were standing hungry.

Shortly after this we made another start; probably we had been hanging about while the troops on the line had been fighting at Glen and Brandfort (the Hants were in that). We moved out towards Winberg and had to go through Hontnek, which the Boers were holding in force. We were on the extreme right

AUSTRALIA

as part of the right flank guard, and moved along a stony ridge, from which we could see all our troops in the plain on our left; on our right were a lot of small *kopjes* and rough ground held by Boers. When the main body came to the *nek* (pass between two hills) they halted, and the infantry proceeded to take the positions on each side—in which they lost heavily, I believe. Meanwhile we halted, of course, and held our ridge.

There was a big farmhouse just under where we halted, with a corrugated iron roof, and we left our horses there and lay out on the *kop*. They had a good try to get our position, and if they had succeeded they might have made it warm for the convoy. We had a hot fire on us, besides two guns with which they soon got our range; but their shrapnel burst too close to us to do us much damage, as it hadn't time to spread. Their guns must have been very close to us, though we could not see them, as the shrapnel burst over us almost immediately after the report of the gun. Those shells that went a bit too far rattled on the iron roof of the farm, making a tremendous row. Altogether, there was more row than damage.

Then we had to go over and clear the hills on the right of the *nek*. We galloped right up on to the position, which was a long hog-backed hill with a *spitz kop* at the end. As the Boers were holding the *spitz kop*, we dismounted and left our horses at a small farm, and advanced on the little *kopje* in the good old frontal attack way at about five paces interval.

That was one of the hottest rifle fires I've been in. I thought it was a certainty of getting hit. You'd see a stone that you were just going to step on spun about five yards in the air by a bullet. Some of the Joes had Martinis, and you'd hear them every now and then—"plonk"—among the ping-pong of the Mausers. There was a common idea that the Mauser always had a double report, but it must only have been against the face of a *kopje* or some condition like that, although I must say I never heard a Martini repeat under any circumstance.

At about a hundred and fifty yards (by this time we were taking cover, and it was bad enough then) the chap next me on the left (Sergeant Ward[1]) got hit by a Martini bullet; he was lying down, and it went in at the top of his thigh and lodged in his kneecap. He was rolling about and swearing like blazes, which was not encouraging, and I was pretty glad when at the next rush we made they suddenly knocked off firing; and by the time we reached the top of the *kopje* they were clearing like one man, so we went back very pleased with ourselves.[2] I waited with Ward till the stretcher party came for him. It finished the campaign for him, for he was sent home—I think they amputated his leg.

Next day we were a sort of patrol away to the right, and were probably the extreme end of the British line. The going was pretty rough, over long sort of table-lands with young precipices (each of which we had to climb up and down), and ravines running through them with thick bush, and generally a farm or two in the bottom. About mid-day we came to one of these farms inhabited. We came right over the top of the bank and on to the farm before they saw us; so I suppose, not having time to clear, they pretended they hadn't meant to. We got any amount of milk, etc., here, and bottled beer, which we hadn't tasted since Aldershot.

Immediately after leaving this farm we spotted a big body of Boers on our right, and I was sent in to Ian Hamilton with the report. They must have been further out than they intended, for I didn't strike the column under a couple of hours' hard riding; in fact, I began to think I must have passed them, and was wondering how long I should be allowed to career around before getting "hands up," when I struck Col. Ridley and his staff, apparently as much on their own as I was. I reported to him, and got the direction of the probable camp (Winberg) and he went off at a tangent again; so there I was "on my lonesome," with the knowledge that there was a town under a blue *kopje* apparently about twenty miles away, where the column would

---

1. I forget whether it was Ward or Hodge.
2. There was an illustration of this affair in the *Graphic*; an officer sent the sketch home.

possibly camp.

I jogged along pretty comfortably, visiting every farm I came to (which were all deserted) till about 3 o'clock, when I came to a big farm. The horse was getting a bit blown, so I dismounted and hitched him up to a gate, and went to explore in the stables. I found any amount of oat-hay, so gave the horse a good feed, and then went in. They had evidently gone in a great hurry, as the place was left quite undisturbed, with all the breakfast things on the table. Coffee, bread, butter, dripping, honey, and preserved ginger. I had a glorious feed, and then had a look round the house. Everything was there: Tante Sannie's best silk dress, all the clocks (one marble one worth any amount of money) and fittings untouched. If I'd had transport I could have furnished a house cheap; but I only took a pillowslip full of flour, and all the portable eatables on the table, including a nose-bag full of sugar!

When I thought I had hung about long enough to be safe-for I was not very sure where either our men or the Boers were—I loaded up the old quad with the spoils of war (to his disgust), and having added a couple of bundles of forage, jogged on towards the *kopje* where Ridley had told me they would perhaps camp. On the road I fell in with another of the 7th, and we entered Winberg together[3] in great style. The troops had gone past the town without stopping, and there were hardly any

MILK AND HONEY

3. The inhabitants (female) were having afternoon tea on the verandas.

military about bar a few staff officers; so we bought a few loaves of bread and a pound or two of butter and sat on the steps of the church and had & great feed. I found the company about 10 p.m.

Next night we were camped in front of a line of *kopjes*, part of which were held by the Boers, and my lot was on outpost. We were supposed to go up on a kop overlooking the Boers' hill, and the major commanding my company (a special service man from home[4]) went out to post us, for it was supposed to be a ticklish place. The company got out all right, and then I had to go on to a *kopje* nearer the Boers as observation post; so three men and myself went off, still with the major, and rode round the foot of our *kopje* and up to the other one and dismounted, leaving one man with the horses.

The major, a Rimington scout who was with us as guide, the remaining two men, and myself proceeded up the *kopje*; the major and scout doing the Buffalo Bill business with drawn revolvers, sneaking from cover to cover and then listening for about five minutes, etc., and the two privates, who were annoyed at being on outpost and sceptical about Boers, stumbling along behind making enough row for a troop.

We got to the top all right, and the major and scout went home after posting us. After about an hour the sentry challenged

THE SPOILS OF WAR

4. Major Colville, A.D.C. to the Prince of Wales, or something.

and unearthed the Rimington chap, who was crawling up to us on his stomach, when he explained that this was the centre of the Boer position—the outpost had gone to the wrong *kopje*!! Then we all did the deer-stalking business back to the horses, and cleared about two miles back to where the outpost had retired to. Of course there was a certain amount of fighting every day, but there were so many troops that they were not all engaged.

The following night we camped in a great open plain with a reedy *sluit* running through. We got in after dark, and were wondering what some lights were that we could see about five miles away, the other side of the *spruit*. I was not worrying much about them, till I heard Major Welch say, "Oh, yes! send Corporal Jackson; he's got the best horse"!

I guessed what he wanted, and tried to ease off to draw the company's rum, or something, till things had blown over a bit; but it was no use, the sergeant-major spotted me, and said, "The Major says you're to saddle up again and go and see what that camp is. He says it's just the thing you'll enjoy." Then he grinned and went to get his supper, after advising me to take a man with me and to come back if it was Boers! I made a mental note to draw a broken-winded horse for my next remount, and then saddled up and warned a lance-corporal, whom I had a grudge against, to come with me. Then we sallied forth into the darkness (another of those d——d romantic situations), and after about three miles of cantering, punctuated by running into wire fences (we had wire-cutters for these) and falling into ant-bear holes, we arrived at the *drift* through the *spruit*. Naturally the *drift* was held by a small party (a troop, I should think) from the *laager* camp or whatever it was. It was a pitch-dark night, and they had not seen us, for there was a rise behind us. This was one of those situations in which the true military genius comes to the front.

I unfolded my plans (slow music) to the lance-corporal: we were to separate and approach the picquet from different sides— thus one of us would escape the fearful carnage! I eased off into the darkness and awaited developments so did the Lance.-Jack!

44

I waited quite a considerable time before it dawned on me that my "gallant comrade" was also a military genius! At last it got too cold, so I advanced gingerly till I got into the *drift* without being challenged, and discovered that it was no outpost at all, but some officers' mess people who had a cart broken down in the *drift*.

Of course, down in the *vlei* we could not see the lights, so we still did not know whose camp it was; these men belonged to Broadwood, but they were not sure how far he had gone, so we had to go on to make sure. As soon as we got close, we could see it was an English camp by the horse lines and men round the fires, so went straight in and reported to Broadwood. He was having a most luxurious late dinner under an awning: table properly laid, silver plate, and lamp shades! His staff with him, of course. We had had nothing since breakfast before daylight, but he didn't invite us; so we went home at the gallop, commandeering some eggs on the way from a Kaffir *kraal*. We had a late dinner on our own after I had reported.

CHAPTER 5

Round Johannesburg

We did not have any more fighting till we got to Sand River. Here we must have eased in to get to a drift or something as we joined the main body, so that there was a pretty big mob of us in front of the drift. The Boers shelled us a bit from some *kopjes* straight behind the drift, but we did not get into it; and after a while they cleared, and we all crossed. We got a few Boer guns which they had left. The Hants were working in the *drift*, making a better place for the transport to cross. Then we had a clear run to Kroonstadt, where we stopped a day or two; and had a visit from some of the Hants, who were lying near—they looked pretty thin.

Lord Roberts inspected all the troops and then Ian Hamilton's Mounted Infantry went off on their own again to Lindley. De Wet had a big convoy here, and we were to capture it; but we took the wrong road or something, and after surrounding Lindley with great caution during the night, we went in next morning to find the town empty, and De Wet lying doggo in the hills towards Bethlehem. We stopped in Lindley (this was the place De Wet had the Irish Yeomanry in afterwards) one night, and then tracked for Heilbron.

The 7th Mounted Infantry were rear-guard, and my company was holding a *kopje* overlooking the town till everything was clear. No sooner had the last troops left Lindley township than Boers were pouring in the other side from every pass and defile in the hills—it is very rough country—and they gave us beans all the way to Heilbron (two days). We would hold a farm and outbuildings till the main body had gone right ahead, and the Boers were working up to within 200 yards, and then mount and gallop like blazes for the next position—pretty exciting, especially if you had an excitable horse that wouldn't let you mount, as some of the men had. As soon as you were away from your cover the Boers were in it!

We had several wounded and some killed: we found the body of one three or four months after, next time we came that way. We left the wounded in Heilbron, and went on for the Vaal. One of the wounded who rejoined us afterwards said De Wet was in there next day, and that he went over the hospital telling the doctors (Germans) to give the wounded anything they required. A doctor offered him a drink of whiskey, but he said: "No, keep it for the wounded." His staff were not so chivalrous, and had a rousing nip each. One of them getting communicative informed a wounded man that he was a deserter from an English cavalry regiment, and seemed rather proud of it.

We were going over great undulating plains now, with an occasional poverty-stricken Boer farm or Kaffir *kraal*, and patches of *mealies* (Indian corn), and great herds of spring-buck, which would get mixed up with the columns and gallop about in long strings looking for a way out. Every now and then the leader would give a bound in the air that would clear a five-barred gate easily, and the whole string followed suit.

Veldt fires were very frequent: We rode for days together over a great black carpet. You can imagine the effect of troops of horse going over an inch of grass cinder; we were all as black as the ace of spades! This is where you get mirages; though the whole ground was burnt grass, every hollow looked like a shallow pool of water, and the troops appeared to be wading through up to their horses' knees.

Mounted men on a skyline appeared to be walking along in the air with about six feet of daylight between them and the ground, and a shimmer of heat over everything. The camps at night in the burnt veldt were glorious. You'd off-saddle and put the horse-lines down with about an inch of fine black ash over everything, then light your fire and sit down in it (the ash, not the fire), get your blanket round you and sleep in it. Next morning you were black enough to polish, and probably no chance of a wash. When we came to the edge of the fire we had to canter through, each man on his own; for it had been a good season, and the grass was up to a mounted man's ankles, so with any wind the flames were well over your head. A good *veldt* fire is a fine sight at night, especially in the mountains.

Just before we got to the Vaal the Orange Free State was annexed. The occasion was of interest to us as we got a double issue of rum.

The daily routine at this time was pretty much as follows:—

Just when you had got comfortably asleep (as it seemed) you would get an uneasy feeling that something unpleasant was happening. As you gradually struggled awake you became aware of your section sergeant, who at that moment was the most unpopular man in the section, coming down the line of saddles—the senior sergeants lived in luxury under the company wagon—shouting, "Come on, show a leg! get these feeds on!" and kicking every figure as he passed.

Well, you stood up ready dressed down to your spurs, yawned like a tunnel, passed your fore-finger round under your coat collar to rake out a little of the sand that the stamping of the horses on the line had covered you with, pulled your Balaclava cap (which had worked round with the opening to the back of your ear) straight, put on your helmet and looked round. If you were of a poetic turn of mind you noticed that the moon was just sinking, making some very pretty light effects on the rises and *kopjes* and on the dam against which you were camped; then you would feel bally cold, and wish the war was over and you were at home in bed; next, you probably observed the section sergeant eyeing you with extreme disapproval, and became aware that all the horses were fed bar yours!

After hurriedly remedying this, you might notice that your mess-mates were also watching you closely, evidently wondering whether you would light the fire. By this time the whole camp would be up, and a great noise of chopping wood and horses munching going on, and little fires springing up all over the place. You probably did not feel keen on lighting the fire, so (if you were a corporal) you became very busy about the men's rations or something in the horse-lines till the fire was lit and the coffee made, when you turned up, rubbing your hands with the air of a man who had begun the day well.

Affecting not to understand the pointed remarks of the three other members of the mess, you would sit down and have breakfast—a billy of coffee and two biscuits and jam, unless you had some private loot, and you were pretty slow if you had not. Before you'd half finished, some officer who had rolled out of bed to a ready-cooked breakfast would be buzzing about energetically, spoiling everyone's digestion, and swearing because the horses were not saddled up. By this time it would be daylight and the outpost coming in.

Probably you, being an unfortunate corporal, were supposed to relieve them, mounted and ready to march off, in which case the sooner you saddled up and got out your three men the less you'd get sworn at. But first you had to roll up your blanket and what kit you had and put them on the wagon; then get mounted and ride out to a rise 800 yards or so off, where you'd dismount and sit on ant heaps and have a quiet half hour, while the column got under way. Probably there would be a few odd Boers hovering about on the sky-line, but they generally waited for the advance screen.

These would move out about sunrise, a company of Mounted Infantry[5] As soon as they passed your post they extended at the canter to about 300 yards between files; then the supports would follow, keeping about 300 yards behind the screen; then the flank guards moved out; presently the whole of the mounted troops in column, then the guns; and finally the wagon convoy, followed by the rear-guard.

When everything was clear you got mounted and cantered

5. Or more, according to the extent of front to be covered.

after your company, reported to the captain, and falling into your place, proceeded at a walk. Presently the advanced screen, which look like black marbles rolling over a russet-coloured carpet, get nearer the low stony ridge where you noticed the Boer outpost in the morning, and you watch them edging up gingerly; then when they get pretty close—flip-flop! flip-flop!—and a couple in the middle dismount and take whatever cover there is, the support gallops up, and some pretty hot firing takes place.

If the Boers will not go for the supports, the general, who is riding along the road with an orderly carrying his flag, and a little group of staff round him, says something to an AJXC, who comes over to your C.O. at the gallop. "7th Mounted Infantry, trot! "and you jog off much to the disgust of a belated private who has been carrying the billy of boiling coffee (which he had no time to drink in camp), in the hope of its getting cool. He hangs on to it till three parts are jogged out and scald his legs; then he flings the remainder away, billy and all if he has a hot temper, and has a grievance for the remainder of the day. Probably the Boers clear after wounding a couple of men and shooting three or four horses, unless they mean fighting, in which case of course the guns come up and the engagement becomes general.

About mid-day, the column usually halted for about an hour—horses were fed (a small feed being carried in the nose-bag), and if the men cared to they could make a drink of tea. At first I used to carry some cold meat and have lunch at the mid-day halt, but afterwards I got used to going without, and just had a light breakfast before dawn and a tremendous blow-out at night, frequently never having so much as a drink all day. I believe this is the healthiest way of living, too; makes you enjoy your supper, anyway.

Then you trekked again all the afternoon, and about dusk the Adjutant calls for markers and canters on to mark out the camp. It's dark by the time you get in, and before you off-saddle the orderly-sergeant reads out the names for outpost. If you are one you swear a bit, get your blanket and strap it on behind your saddle (if it is a mounted post), and file out on the flank, where you are told off to your post. The adjutant probably goes out with you, and you take up your position under a windswept rise, picquet the horses in the hollows, and post your sentry half-way down the other side.

Then you lie down with a blanket round you and eat a couple of biscuits and a bit of bully, and watch the lights of the camp, and wonder whether that thunderstorm on the sky-line is coming your way (if it does, you spend the remainder of the night sitting on an ant heap with half an inch of water round you), and whether there will be a fight tomorrow, and whether they'll send out your issue of rum (probably they won't), till you go to sleep, which you have scarcely done when the sentry kicks you in the back, with "Wot about next relief, Corporal?"

Nothing exciting happened till Johannesburg. We crossed the Vaal without a shot being fired, and about the next day we were skirmishing through some pretty rough country about ten miles to the south of Johannesburg. I was in charge of our advanced screen, and we came suddenly on a farm under a *kopje* with five Boers standing outside. Seeing that they were unarmed I charged the position in great style, and captured them.

Meanwhile the company had stopped about half a mile behind at another farm, and our friends fetched out some bread and meat and a bottle of whiskey, which we finished. Then we discovered their rifles in the house, and took them in to the company. I thought I had done with them; but after skirmishing about in the hills all day we got to camp after dark, about five miles from the farm where the prisoners belonged. I remember there were *veldt* fires all over the shop, and we took a long time to find the camp, for there were lights all round.

I was just off-saddling and looking forward to a feed when Major Welch called me up and told me he wanted me to go back with one of the Boers to the farm to fetch a pony he said he had. I was not to let the Joe go till I had the pony—in fact, not then, as he had not his pass. This Boer was a great, big, strapping old dopper who could have tied me in a knot, only he had no gun and I had, so I didn't mind him much; but I couldn't help wondering whether I should interrupt a tea party at his farm, as there were any amount of Boers behind us. I think it was rather rash of Major Welch, but he'd do anything for a good horse. Well, we shogged off at a regular old Boer amble, I keeping about half a length behind, as I wanted to watch old whiskers.

There was a company left behind in the *kopjes* who did not know where the camp was, and I had to find them on my way and send them in. I told the old chap to make a bee-line for his farm, and he went across country over *kopjes*, through swamps and everything. We happened to strike the company, and I told the Captain (Captain Patterson of the Indian Staff Corps, on special service; he was then in charge of the Norfolk Company Mounted Infantry) to go in. He didn't seem to like letting me go on—I was not much struck with it myself. However, I explained that I had had pretty plain orders, and he went off to camp, leaving me alone in the desolation with my hairy prisoner, to think over all the "little accidents" I had heard of connected with farmhouses.

About a quarter of an hour's jog trot brought us over the spur of a rocky *kopje* on to his farm. I had been trying to draw him as

We set out

52

to whether there were any of his chums hanging round, but he was better at that game than I was, and I did not get much out of him; so as it was pretty late when we got close to the house, and I could see lights in the windows, I proposed that he should go on and prepare his women-folk, in case they were just going to bed. (I knew there was only one door, as I had been there in the morning.)

I took up a strategic position behind a wagon, and watched the door! After he had been in about three minutes, he came to the door and asked me to come in and have some coffee! ! This, of course, was worse than ever, for if there were any men about he had warned them. It would not have done to refuse, as he would have known I was frightened; so I hung up the horse and crawled in with a sort of propitiatory wag of the tail, like Dandy when he used to come into the dining-room without leave. I bucked up a bit when I had a look round, for there was no one there bar my friend, two women, about sixteen youngsters, and a huge fat old *frou* (one of the old *voor-trekkers*, I should think) in bed!

They were all pretty humble, bar the old lady, who glared at me viciously all the time. I didn't stop long, as anyone could see me through the window, and the boy came back to say he could not catch the horse; so I told my friend to give orders for the horse to be sent in to the camp first thing in the morning or he would not be let go; and we started back for camp. The selfish old scoundrel only took one rug for himself, though his four chums were prisoners in camp with no blankets—it was cold, too.

On the way back he was very communicative; seemed in a tremendous stew that he would be sent to St. Helena. He said he had had enough fighting, and wanted to stay at home and "make a little money"—bally old Jew! He was much struck with the big artillery horses he had seen with the column, and wanted to know how much they would cost. I think he was working up to a proposal that I should lift one and bring it back to his farm, but I did not rise.

A FAMILY PARTY

Next day when the horse came in he was given his pass and let go (to be commandeered afresh by the next commando that came along, I've no doubt), and we went on to Johannesburg. There was a lot of noise that day with big guns and pom-poms, etc., but we only struck a corner of the fight. I saw one lot of Mounted Infantry charge a position, and get it pretty hot with pom-poms. I should think there were thirty or forty of them along the line they had ridden.

CHAPTER 6

Pretoria and Diamond Hill

We camped that night on Doorm Kop (where Jameson's Raid ended up, they said), and found a house chock-full of potatoes-had a great feed! We were a long way from water, and I went down to fill the billies for the morning's coffee. When I started back there was a long line of lights on the ridge all round, and I had not noticed which way I had come, so it took me about three hours to find my regiment.

Next day we went into Florida on the Rand, and stayed there while Roberts entered Johannesburg. Then we went through by way of the Kaffir location (where we had a most enthusiastic reception!). Passing through Braamfontein, where the whites brought out bottles of whiskey and all sorts of refreshments, we went out past the show-grounds and camped about three miles up the Pretoria road in a field next a big kitchen garden owned by a German. (The Hants went in with Roberts, and a particular friend of mine was sent in by his colour-sergeant with a lot of money to buy boots for the company.

He got as drunk as a lord, and was finally roped in by the police careering about Johannesburg on an officer's horse that he had commandeered outside the post-office!) That night I was on guard over the kitchen garden, to see the troops did not loot it. I had to go mounted, ready for an early start; so myself and my three men trekked over to the house of the German, who was a well-to-do sort of old chap, and camped down in his back yard, with a flying sentry in the garden. The old chap came out and said if we would look after his garden he would find us in grub. As that was what we were there for I most magnanimously agreed; so he gave us supper that night, and as the troops did not move next day he fed us all day too.

We trekked about 3 a.m. next morning, and I joined the company as they passed. We saw nothing of the Boers till the day we were to get to Pretoria, when we were riding along extended right across country. Ian Hamilton was now on the left of the main body, as far as I can make out. About mid-day there was a tremendous lot of cheering on our right, and an orderly came along and said something to the general. Presently we were halted, and then it was given out: Kruger had left Pretoria, had released the prisoners (which was true next day), and was suing for peace (which was not true at all).

There was great cheering and rejoicing—especially among the reservists, who began conjecturing how long it would be before they were home! Evidently it was believed by the authorities, as we were closed in and proceeding along the Pretoria road in sections of fours. Presently, a big gun was heard in front, which rather disconcerted us, till another one went off; then some genius gave out that it must be peace declared, and they

THE RESULT OF BUYING BOOTS

were firing a Royal salute in Pretoria!

During the first few minutes of the fight at Pretoria Ian Hamilton's mob were walking along the road with their watches in their hands timing the guns! They were pretty regularly fired, too, which helped out the idea; but when the twenty-second went off the reservists' jaws began to drop, and we were hurriedly mounted and trotted off towards the *kopjes* in front of Pretoria. Presently we came on a Tommy shot through the mouth, sitting on the road and looking sulky, and the next turn brought us into it.

We climbed a couple of *kopjes* and careered around a bit without doing any one much harm till about 3 p.m., when we were suddenly called off and collected at the foot of the hills, just any of the Mounted Infantry that they could find (of course in a big scrap troops get mixed up tremendously), and then we galloped right away to the left (our left) for miles, through a pass, then sharp to the right and straight for Pretoria as hard as we could lick. There was only about half a regiment of us then, and when we caught sight of the Fort (Despoort, I think it was

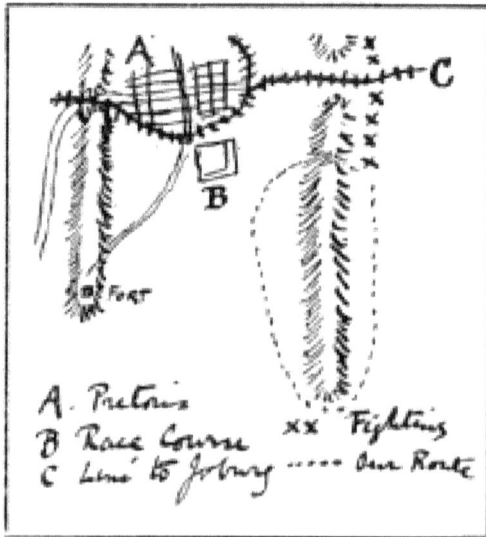

A. Pretoria
B. Race Course   xx Fighting
C. Line to Jo'burg ----- Our Route

58

called) I began to look about for reinforcements, and resolved to cast a shoe if I saw they meant taking Pretoria on our own. However, it appears we were to draw fire from the fort, to see what guns they had; and when we got right opposite the fort we formed up as a British cavalry corps (so they would know who we were) and marched past in style.

I leave you to imagine how we watched that bally old fort. This cats-paw business of drawing fire is a peculiar privilege of Mounted Infantry and mounted troops in general, and we did not like it much; however, they never fired, and we galloped on till we came in sight of Pretoria, just opposite the racecourse, when we turned back into the *kopjes*.

We met the Boer ambulances bringing in their wounded, and a bit further on the water-cart of the Hants Regiment going gaily into Pretoria on his own; he had been looking for the regiment and lost his way. We took him back with us; but the whole of the hills seemed deserted, so we camped down for all we knew in the heart of the defence. That was about the coldest night I had so far, as we had nothing with us, and of course there were no fires allowed.

Next day we joined the main body, and Roberts went into Pretoria. We went up and took possession of the fort we had tried to draw the day before. It is two or three miles from Pretoria, just above a Leper Hospital. It was unoccupied, and had no guns; they had been taken down to Ladysmith. We found a lot of the Staats Artillery and Kruger's Body Guards' uniform in there. We were soon relieved, and went off into Pretoria. Rather an amusing instance of Major Welch's readiness happened on the road.

We had not watered our horses, and we came to a beautiful piece of water; but a sentry was on it, which meant that it was reserved for drinking purposes. However, there was apparently no chance of getting any more, so the Major led us along in sub-sections close alongside the long strip of water. When he saw we were all in front of water, he shouted: "Water your horses! "Of course we wheeled in at once, and were watering before the sentry knew we had turned. He came running up to the Major and told him horses were not to water there. Major Welch looked at him: "What's that, do you want me?"

Sentry repeats his order. Major W.: "Very extraordinary! are you quite sure?"

"Yes, sir!"

"Who posted you here?"

Sentry told him. Major W. kept asking questions and squinting down the line till he saw all the horses had finished. Then he turned to the sergeant-major and said: "Oh, Sergeant-Major! this water is not to be used for horses; get them out at once. Very good, sentry! I'm glad you told me," and jogged off without a smile, swinging his old cane, and muttering "Quite right, quite right! smart sentry, that!" so that the sentry could hear, which appeased him.

We went straight through Pretoria, passing Kruger's house, and camped about five miles the other side. We thought we would stay there for some time, and all the officers went into Pretoria, with the result that when we got a sudden order to trek we left half of them behind; luckily, we went to Trene on the line, so they came on by rail and joined us there. We halted about a day there, and I saw the Pretoria prisoners come down armed with Martinis captured in Pretoria; they garrisoned Trene for a time. Trene is the next station below Pretoria.

We got news that Botha was giving someone (French, I think) beans two days out; so off we went again, and the second day could hear big guns going in front, and soon came on the two big naval 4.7 firing across a valley at some ridges covered with trees. We got orders there, and went on at the canter for about three miles, and took a big, very rough *kopje*.

We stopped up there for about three days, leaving the horses at a farm below. The Boers were on one end of our *kopje*, and there was pretty heavy firing all the time; but not much damage, I think. Now and then about thirty of us used to patrol away out to the front, getting behind the Boers who were on our *kop*, and once or twice had to ride like blazes to avoid being cut off. We might be walking back from some farm that we had been sent to examine, and all of a sudden we'd see a lot of heads bobbing along, just showing over a rise on our flank, going like blazes to try and get between us and the main body. Then, of course, we had to do a bit of Tod Sloan. They never got us.

For these three days we never saw our wagons, so had to feed ourselves: two of us lived on one big pumpkin! We had no blankets either. At last we were called in, and met our wagon on the road. They halted for half an hour, and we had some biscuits and bully, and an issue of rum, and then we started off at a tremendous pace after Botha (he had left his position). But when we had got about five miles they seemed to think better of it, and turned about and trekked straight into Pretoria. That was Diamond Hill, though I didn't know it till long afterwards.

We only stopped in Pretoria a couple of days. We wanted clothes very badly, but could get none; at least, they gave out a few riding pants of the Staats Artillery and some corduroy trousers from stores, but I did not get any. Then we heard we were to go back to the Free State, so at once made up our minds that we were going to do garrison duty in Bloemfontein or some town—we thought the fighting there was all over. Ian Hamilton got us together and we started off south again. We went through Pretoria, and watered our horses in the barracks. The Hampshires were installed comfortably in barracks, much to the disgust, I believe, of the guards and other swell mobs; but we didn't stop long enough to see much of them.

Trekking down east of Johannesburg we stopped at Springs, where I remember it rained very heavily, and I got the fattest sheep I have ever seen; he had a layer of fat two inches thick all over his ribs. We had a brush with the Joes at Heidelberg, driving them over the line. Ian Hamilton got thrown and broke his collar bone, and Bruce took over command. Then at a drift a few miles north of Frankfort I was on rear guard, and we had to wait at the drift till the remainder had got to Frankfort, and some Joes following us up made it pretty warm.

It was a very steep, stony bank, about a hundred yards down

to the drift, and when we retired, by the time we had reached our horses they were on top, and got some nice steady snaps at us going through the river. Then, at Rietz, the best mounted of us took the empty convoy into Heilbron.

At one farm, where we had camped for the night, I remember the old Dutch *frou* came to Tony (Major Welch's nickname) with a complaint about her sheep, which the troops had looted. Tony was just shaving at his Cape cart, and shouting orders, and generally pretty busy and short-tempered, and the old lady planted herself in front of him and contemplated him like a cow looking at a dog. He was a smart, dapper little chap, a great amateur jockey at home, with a quick, fussy temper, and he got rather annoyed. Presently he said, "Well, well, my good woman, what can I do for you?"

She had evidently been primed what to say, as she could not speak English, and she drawled out in a sing-song that the whole camp could hear, "Mine sheep all finish."

"Oh, that's bad!" said Tony; "who do you think took them?"

She had got to the end of her tether, and could say nothing but "Sheep all finish."

Presently he began to get excited, and said: "D—n it all, you don't think I've eaten all your sheep, do you?"

"Ja,"[1] she said, thinking, I suppose, he had asked her if she wanted compensation or something. Of course the whole company started laughing, and Tony was dancing round black in the face with rage; he called his interpreter then.

We got a fresh convoy, and rejoined the main body at Bethlehem. Going through Lindley, that we had been chased out of before, we found the body of the man that had been missing since then, in a *mealie* field. Macdonald was in Bethlehem, and we worked in conjunction with him during the Prinsloo operations (Wittebergen). Bethlehem lies just at the foot of the Drakensberg mountains, and when you go out behind the town you are in the passes and denies at once. Prinsloo and De Villiers and Co. were in the mountains, with only two ways of getting

1. Yes.

out (they said). We were going to stop one way, and some other column the other. Hunter was there, but whether with us or the other mob I don't know.

We moved out to the left of Bethlehem, passing in front of the Range, for a day or two without seeing anything. Then one day I was sent up to the advance guard with a message, and came to a great ravine or canon with a river at the bottom and a great table-land the other side, and behind that the mountains. The advance screen was just starting up the other side, so I scrambled down (it was wonderful the places we could get our old crocks down and up; I really believe that where I could have gone myself I could get my horse) and caught up the advance guard about half-way up the other side.

I went on with them as one of the points in the screen. When we nearly reached the top it came to a gentle slope, so we mounted. It was pretty rough ground, with cracks running down all over the place; and as we got close to the top there were three of us together, and the remainder were round corners out of sight. There was a Kaffir *kraal* on the rise, and as soon as we came over the edge there was a single shot and then a regular volley. We three retired in disorder till we got behind the slope again, and waited for reinforcements!

Presently the Norfolk Company came, very breathless after climbing the cliff, and we rushed the Kaffir village in great style, Brother Boer retiring across a *donga*. We were fighting round that *kraal* for the rest of the day, but there were no casualties in my company. Some of the Norfolks were hit, and we all camped down where we had been fighting. Next day we moved on and drove the Boers over the *donga*, and took up our position along C (see sketch map following).

The infantry moving on our right took the big mountain B, and made the camp under it. We used to go out every day to our position C before daybreak, and come back at dark after being into it all day with shell and rifle fire. We were there for about a week, a pretty exciting time too. It was very cold and wet, with regular tropical thunderstorms.

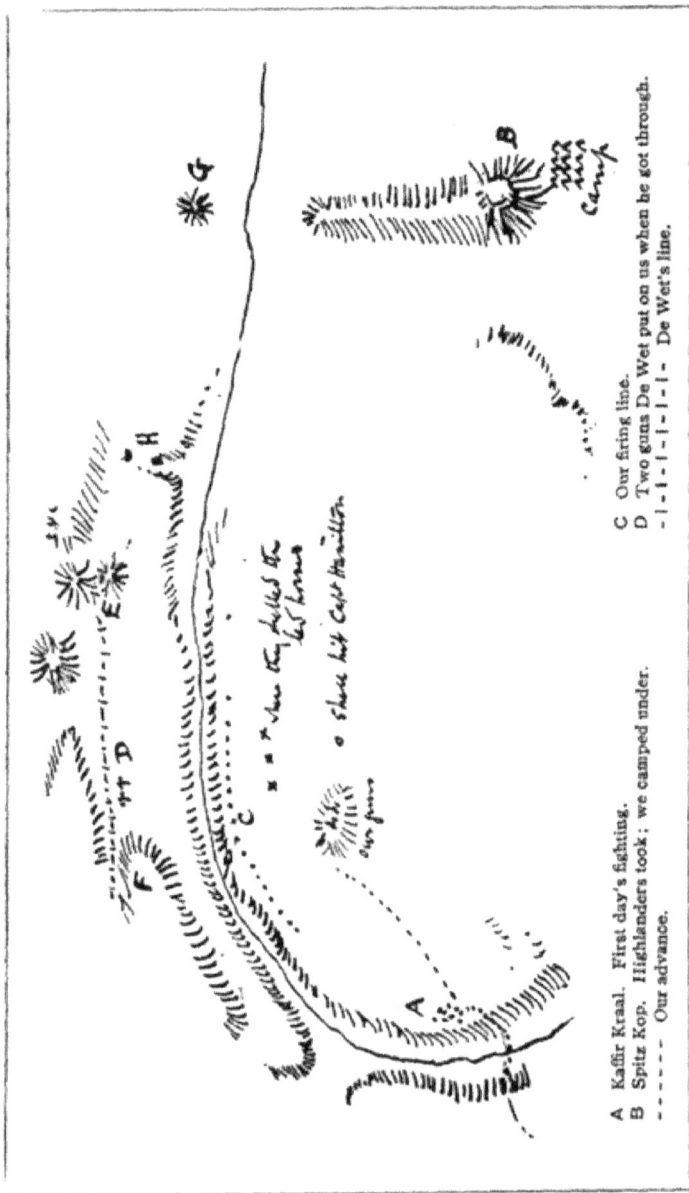

A Kaffir Kraal. First day's fighting.
B Spitz Kop. Highlanders took; we camped under.
- - - - - Our advance.
C Our firing line.
D Two guns De Wet put on us when he got through.
- I - I - I - I - De Wet's line.

G

B
Camp

H

E
F D
C
A

x where they shelled the led horses
o where he[r]e hit Capt Hamilton
our force

We used to be roused out about half-past three, when the cold wind was going right through you, and the old horse looked the unhappiest looking object you could imagine. Then we had to mess about with cold harness, and knock lumps out of our numbed hands with stirrup irons, etc.; then just time for a drink of coffee and file out on the flank, where we had to wait twenty minutes or so shivering while they got the units together; then trek off to the position, which we reached just as dawn was beginning to show, and we'd stamp up and down to keep warm. (I and a Sergeant Murdoch, my section leader, used invariably to pass the time by talking of what hot drinks we would call for if we were in a pub at home!).

Then, as soon as day broke, from the other side of the ravine—"Flip-flop"—and we would have to get down under what cover there was for the day. It kept very cold till about 8, when the sun got some strength; after that, it was quite pleasant lying there all day with the rocks at blood-heat, talking to the man next you, and having an occasional snipe. We were apparently only blocking a pass or something, so we never troubled about pushing the fighting that week.

Sometimes I would stop with the horses, which on this occasion was the worse business of the two, as the firing line were down in loose rocks on the edge of the ravine, while there was no cover for the horses, and they drew most of the shell fire. Each man took four horses and led them back about 600 yards behind the firing line, pretty well out of rifle range. And there

3.30A.M.

65

they were against a smooth green slope, a little bunch of one man and four quads dotted about at about fifty yards distance from each other. Presently the enemy's guns lob over a sighting shot, and for the rest of the day they give different groups fits. I used to sit on an ant-heap and draw up the four horses in front of me and let them have about three shots at me; then if they were coming close, I would move fifty yards backwards or forwards, and so on all day.

Sometimes they'd seem to be betting on the result, as they'd go for our man steadily for an hour, making him move backwards, forwards, and sideways in regular order. It's all right for people to say you ought to stay in one place—it doesn't act when they once get the drop on you; three shells bursting within fifteen yards of you in succession is enough for most nerves. I've known lots of men swear they would not shift again, but three or four shrieking just past them altered their minds. One lance-corporal on my left was sitting on an ant-heap with his horses in front of him, when a shell hit and burst right between the two centre horses and rolled the man over like a rabbit; and yet only one horse was killed.

Once when I was walking back, two of their 15-pounders let off at once, and I could hear them coming for me. One hit just behind the horses I was leading, and burst, hitting a little mare in the hock. As I heard them getting close I had turned round and halted, thinking they were going over, and when this one

SHELLS

66

hit there was a tremendous scuffling; then bang, and the mare squeaked, and all the rest started running round and snorting. I could still hear the hum of the other shell coming, and presently—"Whump"—I heard just beside me, and a great cloud of yellow dust came up all round!

I shut my eyes and humped my shoulders, I can tell you, but it didn't burst; if it had it must have bust me up all right, for when I opened my eyes I was almost standing on the trench it had dug—I didn't wait to see if it was going to burst. Another time one went over me, and Captain Hamilton (of Ridley's staff) came along with a message or something just in time for the bursting of it, and got about eight months in a base hospital, with a lump out of his head. I thought he was dead at first.

Our company was awfully lucky for the best part of the war, for we had comparatively few killed. All the other companies used to have some every day at this time, and yet we all used to work together. We used to say the luck would change some day, and it did in the last six months of the war; but I'll come to that later.

MORE SHELLS

CHAPTER 7

With Macdonald

When we got back to camp we used to have a tremendous blow-out, as that was the only meal of the day, and then a game of nap for *ticky* (3d.) points if it did not rain. Wood for firing was pretty scarce, and I was very proud of the way I got a supply. I'd been away with a despatch or something, and was riding into camp on my own, when I struck a C.I.V. Mounted Infantry man. He was on someone's staff, and he was digging out the only post there was for miles. His horse was just about done, and the post was tremendously heavy, so I thought things looked hopeful, and dismounted and helped him get it out; then he mounted and I helped him up with the log.

Just as I expected, the poor old horse began to give way all round, and he had to drop it; so he wanted me to carry it in and go halves, as it was his pole! Of course I could not think of giving my horse sore withers, so we rode on the half mile into camp together, he intending to get a friend to come out and help him carry it in. I hope they did not go, as I cantered back and got it myself—much to the old horse's disgust!

(Same old crock I started with—still pretty fit; but he looked rough with cold weather and hard times generally.)

That night I remember very well. It started raining about 8 p.m.; and I was sitting over a fire in my big coat till about 10, hoping it would stop. However, it didn't, so I went down the line to my saddle and shifted it back so that I could lie on the dry place it had made, and turned in with a very wet blanket. I was wakened about 12 by a great trampling and splashing, and looking up saw that the horses had pulled up the end peg of the line, and swung round till I was right in the middle of them.

It was still raining hard, but of course I had to get up and fix them up, which wetted both me and my blankets thoroughly through. However, I got in again and went to sleep! In the morning, or rather, at 3 a.m., when it was time to turn out, I felt very hot and stuffy; and when I threw off the blankets and emerged in a cloud of steam, I discovered that the rain had changed to snow, and there was three inches of that everywhere, and a wind blowing that would shave you!

Just imagine turning out at 3 a.m. in soaking wet clothes into three inches of snow and a bitter wind! Talk about the Crimea! The worst part of it was handling your saddlery and rifle; every time you touched a buckle or trigger-guard it knocked a lump out of your hands. Now and then it would be cloudy and blow cold all day, but generally got warm enough about 10 a.m.

About the last time we took up a position at C[1], I think we connived at De Wet's escape. We had been sniping across the *donga* as usual, when we saw a strong body come from E[2], between the two *kopjes*, and advance towards our friends across

THE CAPTURE OF THE POLE

---

1 & 2, See sketch map on earlier page.

the ravine. They threw out advance and flank guards, and the main body moved in column of troops, and we said to ourselves, "That must be Hunter or Broad wood." We watched them cross our front (at a walk) within a mile, and four or five guns of ours covering them never fired a shot, and they went behind F[3]. Just as their rear files got out of sight they wheeled two guns (D)[4], and there were a couple of twinkling flashes and two little puffs of smoke. Before we had time to realise what had happened we heard—"Whom! Whominimi!"—then a screech and "bang! bang! "right into us; and there was a scatter—no one wanted telling to open out in those days. That night, instead of going into camp, we went across to the little *spitz kop* G[5].

We put a few shells into it, and ascertained that it was held (some unfortunate lance-corporal and a couple of men going up till they were fired on), and then back to camp. Next day we went back to the little *kopje*, and while they attacked it our company sergeant-major and myself (I was a sort of odd man, not having charge of a section then) were sent off to the left to watch some rough ground and see that the Boers didn't take us by surprise on the flank.

We got on a rise overlooking a dry *nullah* at about 600 yards, and though the Boers did not come for us, those that our men drove off the *kopje* came along at the gallop by twos and threes, and we had some fine sport all the morning, being for once the snipers instead of the sniped. I hope I hit some, though I can't say I saw any fall!

That night we had a night march, trekking away to the right from the camp at B[6], and about six miles out I was left with ten men on the spur of a mountain till the convoy came up to tell them which of two roads the column had taken; so there I was marooned on a mountain side in a Scotch mist at 10 p.m.! The convoy came along about midnight, and I reported to the chap in charge. He had lost his way several times already, and didn't like wandering about practically without escort he only had about thirty Highlanders with him.

3, 4, 5 & 6. *Idem.*

70

About one o'clock we got on to a tableland, with apparently no way off it except flying, and the major refused to try that; so *laager*ed up. He was in a bit of a stew—with reason, too, for if daylight had showed up our defenceless position to any Boers, we should have been in a hole, and these were the same commandoes that had rushed the Yeomanry at Lindley!

The Jocks lay down and went to sleep under wagons after the outpost had been put out, and I was going to do the same, when the major sent for me and said I was to take my commando on and find the column!! I had last seen them five hours before, vanishing into the mist at the trot, so I did not feel confident; but it was evident something had to be done before daylight. I told him I did not want ten mounted men clattering about the country, and he said I could go by myself if I liked, so long as I went!

So I took one man with a good horse, and we slid, scrambled, and fell down the precipice, immediately finding ourselves in a bog. After scrambling through this we struck a rough *veldt*-track, and as I didn't see any reason for going in any particular direction we cantered along this for about four miles, when we saw a faint light ahead like a burnt-out fire. We then separated, I going well on to the grass on one side of the road and the other fellow on the other side, and advanced gingerly.

Presently, I saw a black figure get up from the fire (where he had no business) and walk towards us and get down behind an ant-hill. I began to get hold of my horse's head in time for a quick turn; but he challenged in English, and we found he was an outpost from the column—which was pure luck, as I had no idea where I should find them. I went back to the convoy, and the major was much relieved to see me. When we found a road down the mountain we came on into camp about daybreak. We had simply made a wide detour and the camp now was behind G[7].

Next day my company went out with orders to clear the two farms H[8], which we did pretty thoroughly; they were simply

---

7 & 8. *Idem.*

bursting with grain and all sorts of produce, and pigs and poultry in hundreds. We wetted all the grain, burnt the forage, and killed the live-stock, leaving merely enough for the family. The women couldn't quite make out Tommy, I think. A soldier, hot and grimy from burning their best haystack, and bloody with the blood of the old *frou's* pet minorcas and anconas, would go up to the back door without a trace of ill-feeling and ask very civilly for a glass of milk, and then proceed to kill the pig!!

I remember our dinner that day. We were burning a wagon and put an iron wheelbarrow on the fire, scraped and cleaned a pig and put him in to fry in his own lard (whole); then, when there was enough fat, filled up the barrow with turkeys, geese, and chickens! and "made it a muck-in" (which is Tommy for sharing), and each man took home as much as he could carry.

A Sergeant Williams was left with a few men, after the company went in to camp that night, to see that all the stuff burnt all right, and for reasons of my own I managed to be left with him. It was pretty dark before we left, and when we got in sight of where our camp should be it was gone! However, we could see lights about five miles on under a hill, so jogged on towards them. When about half-way there we saw another lot of lights away to our left!

Well, we concluded that one was ours and the other Boers, but didn't know which was which, so advanced Deadwood Dick style on the nearest, which turned out to be MacDonald and the Highland Brigade; and we camped down for the night with Lovat's Scouts (who did us very well), and rejoined our column (which was the other lights) next morning.

On the following day we struck straight into the mountain, and had some regular fighting. MacDonald took over the two brigades, and we worked together from now till after Prinsloo surrendered. That morning we were advance guard, and went on before the remainder struck camp till we came to where the road went through a pass between two young mountains. My section went up the right-hand one so as to command the pass, and when we got to the top we found another mountain opposite us higher than our own, with a flat plateau on the top and any amount of Boers riding about on it. (Most of these mountains were tablelands, and when you were once on them you hardly knew you were on a mountain; there were farms up there just the same as below, until you came to the edge and looked down a thousand feet or so on to the plain.)

We had some long range rifle practice while the column went through the pass, and then came down and cantered on ahead again. The Boers had evidently been that way in a tremendous hurry, for we came across broken wagons left with their loads, saddles lying in the road, and all sorts of stuff. Presently we found ourselves in front of Mount Everest, and were told we had to go up. This was no fool of a mountain, and had clouds round the top, so we did not feel keen on it; however, we had to go, and cantered up the first slope till we came to a Kaffir *kraal*, when some Boers opened on us from a road running over a spur. We answered them from the *kraal*, and made the Kaffirs fetch us out Kaffir beer; then dismounted and proceeded up on foot.

Never before or since have I been so convinced of the lunacy of people who go mountaineering in their holidays! We climbed for weeks apparently, and every time we looked up it appeared as far from the top as ever. Every now and then we passed a little stone hut, roughly thatched, just like a peasant's hut in the Slieve Bloom Mountains; in fact, the whole place was not unlike Irish mountain scenery—a sort of bracken growing, and bogs where little tricklets oozed out of the rocks.

Well, we tailed off as we went up, till we were straggling for a quarter of a mile from the top. Just at the top was a sharp shelf, and then the usual tableland stretching away as if there was no such thing as a mountain about. Fifteen of us climbed over the shelf together and lay down puffing and swearing, too blown to remember anything about Boers; but they soon reminded us. On the plateau about 400 yards from us was a low stony ridge, and as soon as we threw ourselves down—Whiz-whiz-phit!— all round us, and to see us break for cover you would never have dreamt that we had just been done up with climbing! One man was hit in the back (he died), and another in the knee, and as I was doing a sprint over the edge of the bank I got a sharp vibration in the rifle, a bullet just grazing the barrel. The remainder came up, and an hour or so afterwards the led horses arrived, and we stayed on the edge all the remainder of the day, keeping up the sniping at the Boers, who were reinforced pretty heavily.

We slept up there that night. My section-sergeant, myself, and six men being sent along to where there was a sort of spur, as outpost. Before light next morning, all the remainder moved off round the mountain, leaving us behind as a draw. We felt pretty forlorn: eight men on a mountain top, with an unknown quantity of foes within 400 yards. We had to hold the place as long as possible, and then clear in the direction the remainder had gone, and chance it whether we found them or not.

We kept up as heavy a fire as possible, to make them think we were all there still; but there were about sixty of them, and they sent two men round a spur that overlooked us, and we thought it was good enough to quit, so sent our horses down to where we could ride round a slope, and then waited. Between us and the Boers, about a hundred yards to our front, was a row of stone posts, and the Boers started working towards them. Sergeant Murdoch sent me and three men out to take possession. It was going to take some time to get the horses down the rough bit; so we skirmished out, and each got behind a post and blazed away while the Boers were chipping lumps out of our cover.

I knew they would rush as soon as the men got back who had been round our flank, and was never more pleased in my life than when the sergeant called us in. We made a bolt for it, none getting hit, straight over the edge and down the hill, about fifteen yards at a stride, to the horses, and got round the corner of the slope all right. We could hear big guns going on another mountain, so made for it, and picked up the company about mid-day. They were on a little *kopje* on the plateau, having a lot of shooting with Boers, on a skyline about 300 yards off, and as we galloped across the open to join them we got it pretty hot.

We were on that *kopje* all day, and a captain of the K.O.S.B. was hit in the side just below the heart. They got him down to camp, but he died in the night—Wilkinson, I think his name was—and three or four men were hit, too.

Just before dark all the Boers cleared down the mountain and rode off towards Harrismith. We got a splendid view of them going like blazes, just like a hunting crowd breaking away from the Hemplow! You could hear the chaps all over the mountain whooping away as they viewed them.

We retired then, going down a place like the side of a house. My horse used to shut his eyes and hold one foreleg out straight, and then gradually go forward till he over- balanced and went down about six feet; then he'd grunt and have a look round. As we were riding along the road towards the camp we came on a Boer lying in the road with the whole top of his head blown off—he had been hit by a shell.

After that we had a day off while negotiations were going on, and a couple of Boer envoys came in to MacDonald. It was two of my company from the outpost line who brought them, and they said MacDonald bullied the two Joes till they didn't know whether they were envoys or prisoners. When the surrender was arranged we saddled up and moved off *en masse*, with a white flag in each unit to show we were not attacking.

After we had gone about eight miles without a sign of their *laager*, it seemed to strike the general that it was a trap, for all of a sudden the white flags were taken in and we were thrown out in skirmishing order. My company was on the extreme right, and we had to go up every ravine and defile to our right, searching the country for the bally old *laager*. By this time we were all convinced that it was a trap, and I believe that the men who did happen to find it cleared back at the gallop and waited for reinforcements.

However, it was all right, and when we went in we found the whole lot drawn up in line, each man squatting in front of his horse, and all the rifles and bandoliers stacked. We camped alongside them, and everyone who had a bad horse had to go and change with a Boer. They had all the Irish Yeomanry horses with them, and they were a fine lot—English and Irish hunters. But I wouldn't have changed my old quad then for a thorough-bred; he lasted out most of those we got there.

These last illustrations of mine are wrong; as a matter of fact, as we were not clothed like that at this time, one could hardly have told the majority of us from Boers. Most of us had corduroy pants that we had looted from stores, and a good many had prison clothes with O.V.S. stamped on them (Orange Vrij Staat), which we got from Frankfort prison. I believe I was about the only man in my company with a decent pair of riding breeches, and those I bought from the Malta Mounted Infantry just out from Malta. A lot of men wore strips of blankets for putties, and some none at all.

One man, I remember, had a pair of woman's clocked stockings (looted from some farm), and he used to draw them up over the knees of his riding breeches and ride along quite pleased with himself. Altogether, what with being lean and hard, unshaven and more or less dirty, we were a pretty tough-looking crowd, and the horses grew long rough coats in the cold weather, and the contrast between this and the painted picture of the

THE RAGGED M.I.

Mounted Infantry as they started from Bloemfontein must have been pretty striking.

Pretty well every man of this capture was provided with a horse of sorts and rations to last him to his home and was let go after taking the oath of allegiance. This lasted them until, as he puts it himself in his book, De Wet "conceived the great plan of calling back to the commandoes all those who had been allowed to return to their farms on taking the oath of allegiance"!!!

AFTER A YEAR

CHAPTER 8

From Harrismith To Heilbron

Still with MacDonald we trekked to Harrismith. MacDonald was not fond of the Mounted Infantry, and was always sending us insulting sort of messages. For instance, if we were in front, he would send up to say "if that d———d Mounted Infantry kicked up such a dust in front of his men he would dismount them and give their horses to the Highland Brigade "; and after that we used to keep behind, when he discovered that we caused too many veldt fires by men dropping matches smoking, etc., and there was another order that if there was another fire he'd dismount us all.

That night it happened that his precious Highlanders had a tremendous fire in camp, and MacDonald had the cheek to send for the Mounted Infantry to put it out for them. He heard some pretty straight talking then, and I suppose he thought he had gone far enough, for he left us alone till we reached Harrismith.

This is a nice little town right in the Drakensberg Mountains. We camped about three miles out, and MacDonald gave out that "the people of Harrismith came of decent Scotch descent, and anyone looting, etc., would be hanged," and all the rest of it. We thought the "Scotch descent" was pretty good. We stayed there about a week, and the people who were by way of being loyal, used to drive out in the afternoons to look at us—we were the first troops who had been there.

About the second night I was told off to go down to the town and take charge of a mounted picket (the N.C.O. in charge had been made prisoner or something), so I saddled up and went down. I passed the pickets coming home at the trot, but wanted to see the town, so went on and had a look round.

Just as I was getting back to camp I saw a procession carrying sacks of *mealies* across some ploughed land. This wanted seeing to, so I rode over and discovered our company sergeant-major and a lot of men he had collected, dumping bags of *mealies* by the dozen from a little tin shanty, so I turned to and helped, and we were carrying in in the moonlight half the night. Our horses lived on it for weeks after. There was a deuce of a row about it, but I don't think old MacDonald ever knew who had it.

We stayed at Harrismith about a week, and several of the sergeants, the company sergeant-major, and myself used to go down and have great dinners at a hotel where there were some very pretty girls—daughters of the house. Then we trekked back to Lindley, and from there to Heilbron. Between Lindley and Heilbron we had an exciting time. It is two days' march, and the first day we were riding along pretty unconcernedly, my company close in to the convoy, when a man came in in a hurry from the advance guard, and MacDonald and his staff galloped up to the head of the column.

We thought something must be up, but heard no firing or anything; however, presently an orderly came back for us at the gallop, and we had to go up to the front. Still no sign of anything, but we were formed as an advance guard between the proper advance guard and the column. We were advancing along the road now, and about 1,600 yards on our right flank was a range of hills, or rather *kopjes*, running parallel to the road. Next we got the order "trot," then canter (though an Mounted Infantry trot generally is a canter), and just as we were wondering who was mad and if we were going to attack the advance guard, we got "right wheel!" and we wheeled and went for the *kopjes* as hard as we could lick.

We had scarcely started the wheel when old Olivier, who was lying doggo in the *kop*, thinking we had not spotted him, saw the move, and before two sections were round he had about five shells into us, the first going well over, and the remainder, some bursting over and some hitting amongst us. I was on the extreme left, and the line drew through a bit of a *nek* on the right and made for a kop about 800 yards from the Boers, so that I was left a bit, and when I came our men were going up the *kopje* as they arrived.

Just as I got to the foot one of their shells burst about 40 feet in the air, and I saw a black thing come buzzing down towards where I was just handing over my horse to a No. 3. I watched it come, and saw a red gash seem to jump out on an old grey mare's leg; then the black thing struck and bounced with a hum about 600 yards. The mare had her kneecap sliced clean off—it must have been the cap of the shell.

I went up to my section, and we had some pretty heavy shell fire for about twenty minutes—good cover, though! By this time the infantry and artillery were out from the convoy, and there was some pretty hard hitting as the infantry attacked the whole line of *kopjes*. Presently we got an order to get right away to the rear of the convoy, as the Boers were working round the right of the firing line and threatening the column; so we mounted and went off right along the whole length of the firing at the gallop, and had a good view of things.

One regiment (Derbys, Essex, or something) had gained a spur on the *kopje*, and had a pom-pom on them. They were getting it pretty hot. We could see them hopping about from stone to stone, and I noticed a lot of men being carried and helped back. They lost about thirty killed, we heard afterwards. We didn't wait to see details, though, especially as we came in for anything that got past them. Then we struck a gun coming up at the gallop to within 300 yards of the *kop*. Just as we passed them a pom-pom shell cut a poor old gun-horse's hoof right off above the coronet.

He was an off-sider, and the driver blew his brains out, cut him out, and they were under way again before we passed them, and we were galloping. We passed the A.L.I., and then seemed to be galloping off right away from the fight. For about two miles we went, along the direction we had come from Lindley. One man in my section swore his horse was done up, and got leave to go back to the column. The men seemed to think he was scared of being cut off, as we were only one company. If that was his reason he didn't gain much, as he was cut off on his way back, and shot through the neck—he was invalided by it.

Presently they opened on us from a ridge in front; so we knew we had struck the party we were after, and dismounting left our horses in a *mealie* patch. We went on about 300 yards and lay down on the open *veldt* with no cover at all, and started answering the rifle fire—this was all right!

I was never much worried by rifle fire unless it was very close, but the old range of *kopjes* ran along still about the same distance from our left flank (about 1,600 yards), and they detached a gun for our special benefit, which took up a position in a little *nek* at right angles to our line as we lay down, so that we were engaged with rifle fire in front and enfiladed with shrapnel on the left, and no cover. I never agreed so much with the Czar's disarmament proposals as I did all that afternoon.

They got the exact range in two shots, and kept on at regular intervals, dropping a shell a few feet in front or rear, and now and then between the files (we were extended to about fifteen paces). Sergeant Murdoch was lying on my left and Lance-corporal Dale on my right. One shell hit right against Murdoch's ("Binks" we used to call him) heel and half buried me in red sand. Then three in succession hit just in front of "Billy" Dale— after the third he moved about ten paces back into the *mealies*, and I'm hanged if they didn't miss him by about eighteen inches next shot. He went back into the line looking a bit white about the gills.

I felt kind of seasick myself. I always did hate shrapnel, but "Binks" seemed rather to enjoy it. I used to keep firing to my front, and after three or four shots I'd look furtively over to the *kopje* and there would be a little white cloud all right; then after an age of waiting I could hear the hum of the shell and the dull "bump" of the report, and the closer the shell came the closer I'd squeeze myself to the ground till I heard the bang and looked up to see where it would hit; then just as I was recovering there'd be the little white cloud again, and the same sensations all over again. All the afternoon this kept up, and I was pretty sick of it.

I think that idea of novelists about the officers walking about under fire and showing coolness, being a good thing to keep men steady, is all rot. We had a young sub. who used to belong to the C.I.V., and he had evidently read Kipling or someone's yarns of that sort. He sat on an ant-heap with a black great-coat on (against a russet background) and smoked cigarettes ostentatiously, probably thinking he was encouraging the men.

They didn't take it that way though, and the remarks would have surprised him if he had heard them—"Sergeant, tell that . . . young idiot to get down, he's drawing all the fire in the Free State," and so on. Besides, I never knew a case; for rather on the average the men want no more steadying than the officers, and, as a rule, the officer knows what is going on and where he can retire to, etc., which the men never do, so they want more nerve if anything, I take it.

Two or three men were hit of the Malta Mounted Infantry, I think, but none of my company, and we retired by companies. When it was nearly dark they got a pom-pom on us as we were crossing a *mealie* patch, but did no damage; and we couldn't find the camp for a long time, as the shells had lit the veldt and there were lights all over the place. My company was last retiring, and we nearly got rushed just at dusk. The company in front of us shouted to us just as we were going down one of the undulations, and our rear-guard came up at the gallop with about sixty Joes on their track. We just opened out in time. They emptied their magazines at us and cleared as the front companies were coming back—only hit a horse or two. The ambulances were out all that night. Altogether it was quite a respectable little mix-up.

We got into Heilbron next day, and I'm hanged if MacDonald did not give out that he considered the troops wanted bucking up, and he was going to carry out spring drills, starting at 6 a.m. next morning! At "spring drills" you go through the whole routine that a recruit does—goosestep, saluting by numbers, etc.—so imagine the feelings of the men who had not been drilled since Cork! We did one hour in the morning, and then Ridley, who was in command of the Mounted Infantry, moved us all out about ten miles, for grazing, I think the excuse was, which relieved the pressure. That was the last time I worked under MacDonald. I was not sorry either. After a couple of days we went off into Kroonstad, leaving the Highland Brigade in Heilbron.

CHAPTER 9

Adventures With Remounts

The next year I have got rather mixed up, as we kept going round over the same ground—that is from Lindley in the north to Aliwal North on the Orange, and from the line to the Basuto border. I know every road and drift in that tract, I believe; but I will work it out as far as I can remember, or rather I will give the interesting bits.

It was about this time that we were drafted to Le Gallais' column, with the Malta Mounted Infantry and several other mounted corps, 5th Mounted Infantry and Burmah Mounted Infantry among them. There were not many of the Burmah ponies left by this time, but they were a fine body of men—all two-badge men almost, from the regiments stationed in Burmah, Durhams, Essex, etc. After messing about round Winberg district for a bit, we struck off down the line to Ventersburg.

The day we got there I was on the extreme left wing, and as they kept wheeling to the right I was cantering practically the whole way. I thought the old horse would not last much longer, as he was going very thin and starey about the eyes, and this day finished him. He fell heavily once and shook me up a bit, and after that I could feel the difference; it was like the feeling you get from a sprung racket when he was cantering.

It was a long day, and we did not strike camp till dark. The poor old beggar hung on till he saw the camp and then stood and shook all over, and it took me about two hours to get him half a mile. Next day we went in to Ventersburg Road Station, and I had to lead him in. A party went down from here to Bloemfontein with sick horses, myself amongst them. I used to ride on a wagon and let the old horse go on his own. The regiment passed us going down by rail (it was the time of the Ladybrand siege, and they were going out on the relief).

When we got to Bloemfontein I found some of our men already there at the remount camp, and they said the company Sergeant-Major Weston was in hospital, having been left when the company went out to Ladybrand. When he came out we had great times for a few days. He and I used to go down town for our meals, and all we had to do was to feed and water the sick horses. We generally went for dinner to the railway dining-room, as that was the only place where you could get beer; and one day we were sitting at our table, when there was a bit of a scuffle, and a lot of staff officers came in for lunch off the down train from Johannesburg.

This was Baden-Powell. I thought I was having too good a time to last long, and when we had had about three days there (theatre every night, swimming baths, etc.), an order came for all the available men to take out a convoy of Cape carts with forage for the troops at Ladybrand (which they had relieved), so I had to go in charge, as the sergeant-major had no one else. He stayed in charge of the sick horses.

I got together about thirty men of various corps who were loafing about Bloemfontein, and marched them with a blanket a man over to the transport lines, where we arrived at about 10 p.m.—no rations or anything—so we had to camp down till morning, when they took us down to the mule lines and told each man to grab two mules. Then each was given a rickety old Cape cart, and we had to file off and load up with oats. I pulled out about 3 p.m. and camped at the first water, near Bushman's Kop; so don't forget I once had sole command of a convoy.

The road was along a line of block-houses, and there were all sorts of people travelling along: officers going in or out of Bloemfontein on leave; troopers who had lost their units and were very much afraid of finding them again, etc. It was about a

I dine with Baden-Powell

three days' march, and I had mules dying about every five miles. If there was another mule or horse in sight I stole it, if not I distributed the load amongst the other carts and burnt the cart.

One night, at a place we called Siege Hill (because we were held up there for some days afterwards), I had outspanned and dished out feeds for my sixty-four mules and rations for my thirty-two men, when I sighted a tent all on its own by the side of the road, and a Cape cart and a lot of horses grazing all round. Well, I was all right for horses at the time, but I had several timed to die about mid-day next day, so I sent a chap of the Leicester Regiment to bring two of these. He belonged to the Mounted Infantry, so I thought he knew how to steal a horse; but apparently he thought I'd bought them, for he went straight up and took them from in front of the tent.

I did not see him, and thought everything was all right, till we were all having supper and I heard a "staff-officery" voice inquiring who was "in charge of this damned caravan." I guessed what was the matter, and would have resigned my command on the spot if possible, but when I went up to him he already had the man who had stolen the horses, and was asking him if he knew the penalty for looting was death, etc. I thought things looked pretty cheerful. However, after he had frightened the man considerably, he changed his tone, asked him if he thought he was d——d fool enough not to watch his horses when there were any thieving Mounted Infantry about, and finally swore that each horse had a blanket on (which he had not), and if he did not return the blankets as well he'd run him in for horse-stealing! So the unfortunate chap had to go and steal two blankets to square himself.

After this the old chap—he was Colonel Ridley, retired of some Hussars, who was out in command of a Yeomanry lot-got quite friendly, had a drink of coffee with us and told us all sorts of yarns about his soldiering days. He bragged like blazes about what he had done in the war, swore he captured Olivier himself—it was his yeomanry that got him, I believe—and promised to get me into the Hampshire Police Force if I went to see him after the war; said he lived at Winchester, and when he went back to his tent sent us over some papers with an account of the capture of Olivier!

Next day we caught the column, and I handed over my convoy to the commissariat and joined my company, and the day after we started off up country at a tremendous pace after De Wet or someone. I was given a big Argentine which had broken down once and had been trekking with the wagons for a rest, and about the third day's trek we were away in front of the left flank going like blazes after some wagons and Cape carts, when he broke down again and stood with his legs apart and not a move in him.

The company went on and I was left alone on the *veldt*. I ought to have shot him to prevent the Boers getting him, but let him off and left him standing looking after me—pretty forlorn he looked, but there was plenty of grazing and a dam near, so I expect he was rolling fat in a fortnight. But I had to carry the saddle and bridle in to where I judged the column would pass. Luckily I hit them all right, and got on our company wagon. The company did not turn up till early in the morning. They had had quite an exciting little bit of night work, and had captured several Boers and Kaffir scouts.

I never had much use for being dismounted, so early in the morning I went over to the prisoners and found, as I expected,

DISMISSAL OF THE ARGENTINE

they still had their horses; so I marched straight up and took one of the Kaffir's, and the guard never said a word, evidently thinking I would not do it without some authority. It was only a little rat of a pony, and after the first day I swapped with the man in charge of the water-cart, as anything would do riding along with the convoy, and got another Argentine.

After this came a few weeks of hard trekking and sniping. Le Gallais was a great man for early starts. We were generally well on the road before sun-up, and he used to make us walk a good deal, leading the horses—which was good for them but unpleasant for us, as riding all day and every day is not good practice for marching. I remember we called in at Heilbron, and then struck up north, hitting the line at Vredefort Weg station, where we saw Mr. Mann of ours, who was intelligence officer there. Then we went down by the line to Kroonstad, and camped in a very pretty place by the river, all among trees. You can imagine what that is after you've been living in glaring sun for months, and seldom getting a chance of a wash, much less a bath.

I forgot rather an amusing incident that happened when we were at Heilbron. Two or three of our chaps went out to a farm about four miles out, for firewood, which was very scarce there. They got an old Cape cart, practically nothing of it but wheels, and hitched in their horses by their stirrup leathers, and putting a couple of long fence poles on the cart started for camp. They had been watched all the time, apparently, as directly they started back a dozen or so Boers came after them as hard as they could lick.

When they began to get in rifle range our chaps saw they could not get away with the Cape cart, so halted to outspan, which they were doing in a deuce of a hurry (they were hitched in with string and all sorts of contrivances), when on one of them looking up to see if the Joes were getting close, to his surprise they had turned tail and were clearing as fast as they had come! No one else was in sight, so they must have taken the old Cape cart with the fence pole sticking out for a gun, and thought they had halted for a shot. Those men called themselves

"No. 4's Gun Section" after that! Our company was "No. 4" of the 7th Mounted Infantry.

We had a great lot of men in the company at this time; d——d good men in a row, but scoundrels to the backbone. Great gamblers, too—some of them used to sit up all night round a bit of candle in a blanket bivouac, gambling. "Banker," "brag," etc., and earlier in the evening "crown and anchor" boards, "under 7 and over 7" was going all over the camp. The Burmah Mounted Infantry were tremendous gamblers, too, on a pay night, which did not occur very often. The camp would sound like a racecourse or fair—everything dark, except little patches of light from the mess fires and spots of light visible between the legs of the men crowding round some worthy with a "crown and anchor" board, and just the dim outline of the horse lines.

All round you'd hear them shouting like bookies: "Roll up, my lucky lads," "Patronise the old table," "The only chance the old man gets," "The lucky old seven," "This time, gentlemen."

Further on they'd be playing a weird sort of game called "House," played with numbered cards, with an outlandish jargon of its own—"House abaht," "Kelly's eye," "Top of the house," "House on the top line"! etc. Pretty big sums were won, too, but generally lost next night. I've often seen a man draw about £3 on pay day and go to sleep with over £50. The men who "kept" the boards, or were "banker" at cards, were generally flush enough, though!

I used to patronise the "crown and anchor" boards most, in a mild way, as there is no brain work about it, and I was never any good at cards. I suppose you'll be surprised that it was not

"Coffee" Oakford   Sims

90

stopped. It would have been jumped on at once at home, but a lot of irregularities like that came to be allowed after about a year's trek, which accounted for a lot of trouble for us later on; but I'll come to that.

To return to Kroonstadt. The old Argentine that I got from the company, Bhisti, was no use at all, and I got leave to get a proper remount here, which was the second horse I had (you couldn't call the two Argentine remounts, as they were both done up before I got them). I and a chap called Page, who was good at talking Hindustani, used to go down to the remount depot, which was run by a regiment of Bengal Lancers (Captain Patterson's regiment, I think), and have great yarns with the *ressaldars, jemadars*, etc.

When the remounts came up I spotted a thick-set, cobby little mare. I'm not sure what nationality she was, but she looked very fit, with a beautiful fine coat too fat, but we would soon alter that. I got the sergeant-major to give her to me, and was pretty pleased with myself. She was about five years old, and you could do anything with her—play about with her any way you liked. I used to go and lie down on her full length when she was lying down, and she'd only grunt. I used to call her "Betsy," as she was just like a fat old cook in her ways. I sent another chap down to water with her, and they were all laughing when they came back. He said, "You've got a capture in that mare." I didn't think he was talking sarcastically, as no one said anything.

Next morning we were to march, and as luck had it I decided to take my big coat and had it strapped on in front. There was a lot of excitement that morning; there were a lot of remounts, Australians mostly (I think mine must have been an Australian, though she was not a whaler type to look at). When the order was given to mount, the fun began—horses bucking all over the place.

Most of the Mounted Infantry men at this time could ride as well as anybody else, but, of course, had not been accustomed to this. You'd see a man stick it for about four bucks, amidst great excitement and many bets on him or the horse, then he'd lose his stirrups and next grab the saddle behind with one hand, and at last he'd have to come down or the saddle would go round. Some few, however, sat as if they had been brought up to it, and after bounding all round their company would get in their places all right. I had a horrible suspicion, and looked at the old mare; but she was standing with her fat legs braced out, and her eyes half shut, breathing heavily and looking such a blowsy old reprobate that I thought it was impossible that she could misbehave herself in that line.

Well, we got mounted and moved off at the walk, the mare bucking up a bit and sidling along with a fat, rollicking sort of stagger, and I thought things were looking all right. Then we got the order to trot, and things began to happen. I was a *serre-file* at the time—that is to say, I rode behind the line of my section—and there were about three companies in front of us all in column of sections. When the mare heard them drawing out in front and saw the dust rising, she put her head up and looked interested; and when our company started to trot, I had an instinctive feeling that it was my turn to amuse the troops.

I can remember taking a few odd turns of the reins round my wrists, and trying to lock my toes under her girth (no good, she was too fat!), and then, when my section started off, she seemed to think that this was the time she'd star. She gave one buck leap through the section, brushing the bony old Argentines and Cape ponies aside as if they didn't count, cannoned between the officer and sergeant-major, and went up to the head of the regiment, "like the divil wint through Athlone, in standing jumps." I didn't have time to see much, but I have a confused recollection of mingled laughter, jeers, encouragement (mostly ironic), and curses from those I hit; and every fifteen yards or so there would be a shock and fresh commotion as I struck a new section.

The only way that I knew how I was getting on was by the different dialects, from the "Hooray, stick it Peter!" of our's to "Mon, whar the de'il are ye gaein'?" of the K.O.S.B. The old lady was pretty good; she caught me after each jump very cleverly, but it was pretty painful. I pulled out before I got up to the

C.O., luckily, and waited for the company; the old mare looking rather pleased with herself, in a good-natured sort of way. She always used to get herself as untidy as possible.

If I let her go for a few minutes' graze at a halt she would roll so as to get the saddle half round her belly and rub her bridle till it got over one ear and eye; then she'd get one leg through the reins and stand there as happy as possible till I went and unravelled her. She treated me to the above every day for about a week, when she settled down, evidently thinking that twenty miles a day was enough without extras.

Another favourite game of hers was to refuse to water at a dam or deep pool till there was a tight ring of horses round it drinking, when she'd lob one ear forward and flounder in shoulder over shoulder to see how many she could knock in, and then she'd stand contentedly sucking in water and dribbling it all out again, listening to the language. She always used to remind me of a drunken woman with her bonnet on crooked.

We started burning farms on this trek along the Valsch River, and had a little sniping, but not much. One man of the Lancers (who were with a column that was working with us, probably De Lisle) got in the range of a Maxim that the Joes had, working under forced draught, and nearly got cut in two, and we had several more wounded, whom we left at a farm with a R.A.M.C. orderly. We got a yarn afterwards that the Boers shot them all, but I don't believe it was true, though no doubt they were riled at the farm burning, not being used to it then.

Amusing the Troops

CHAPTER 10

Bothaville

I am not very clear where we went after this, but we must have circled round to the north,

I think, as I remember next being camped at a siding on the line just opposite Rhenoster Kop in one of the worst rains we had. At this time we had no tents or shelters of any kind. You could make a blanket bivouac with two rifles if you liked, but it was no good for rain; so we just used to crawl under a water-proof (?) sheet and stick it out. It rained all night, and next morning it was still raining. A party of casuals joined us here from depots, hospitals, etc. One of these, Sergeant Henson, brought a remount with him. This he kept till peace was declared, which is a record that I doubt if anyone has beaten—he was a country-bred, though. He got shot through the neck afterwards, but never stopped trekking. We trekked out about

2 p.m. towards Rhenoster Kop (still raining), and when we got to it a few of us had to go and draw fire (if there was any). It was rather a nasty place—a great stony *kop* covered with bushes and with old shafts all over it where they had been prospecting, and a thick fringe of bush round its base. However, we climbed all over it and saw nothing but guinea-fowl, so joined the column which was camping about two miles the other side, about half a mile from the river bank.

It was just about sundown, and a more miserable prospect you couldn't imagine—a long stretch of ridges fading away in the drizzle to a dead grey skyline, Rhenoster Kop looking hazy through the rain, and the river with desolate-looking bush on the banks. Add to this every solid thing wet through and the camp like a quagmire with the horses and mules trampling it, and absolutely no shelter or dry wood, and you've got one pretty good reason for cursing the war, and the country, and everything else that catches your attention.

We had just got the horses on the line and were standing about trying to light fires and to find a dry place for our blankets, when about a dozen sportive Joes appeared on the line of the nearest ridge and emptied their magazines into camp.

Some energetic people turned out after them, headed by "Tony" Welch swinging his cane, and they cleared, to spend the night comfortably in one of the farms along the river. One horse on our line was hit through the fetlock. I spent the night on an ant-hill, and it was still raining in the morning when we had to paddle about and mess with sopping saddlery and a drowned rat of a horse at 4 a.m.!! (Happy day!) We trekked along the river bank. While one chap was climbing his horse up the steep slippery bank, his whole outfit went backwards through thorn bushes into the river, which bucked the remainder of us up a bit. But we didn't see the sun till next day, so were wet through all the time.

The next thing I remember was being camped on the Valsch, near Bothaville, and, going down for a swim, seeing the major of the Burmah Mounted Infantry save a chap from drowning. Next day we went and burnt Bothaville, taking what inhabitants there were with us, and struck due north towards Potchefstroom.

One day I was on right flank guard, and one of my points called me over to him. He had found an old prospecting shaft half-full of tin boxes and furniture. We went through it. (At this time we would not have taken anything bar eatables if the Joe had left the things in his house.) Most of it was clothing, but the other man got two watches, and I got a double-barrelled shot gun, which I carted round on our wagon for months till the wagon broke down and the rear-guard burnt it.

We crossed the Vaal at Schumann's Drift. I was rear-guard,

and there were several snipers behind us following us up. It was a hot day, and I had my coat strapped on behind my saddle with my diary in it, which I had kept up till then; also my purse, with what was left from the last (distant) pay-day. The strap came undone, and I lost the coat. I thought it was not good enough to go back looking for it.

The Potchefstroom side of the Vaal is all *kloofs* and *krantzes*, a great place for baboons. There is a gold reef running through the chain of hills and a little mining town, Venterskroon. De Wet was by way of being "completely hemmed in "here, and we and De Lisle were to walk in and squelch him. After we crossed the Vaal we went like blazes along a bush road between two lines of *krantzes*, till we came out on the open plain overlooking Potchefstroom.

We had overrun the trail, so struck back to Venterskroon, where we had a mid-day halt. (I have been all over there since the war, and if we had climbed the great *kopje* over Venterskroon, as I heard the officers debating whether it was necessary to do or not, we should have looked down on De Wet's outspan in Buffel's Kloop; but we did not, so he lasted out to make a good many "regrettable occurrences.")

After an hour or so we recrossed to the Free State side over Venterskroon drift (this morning's trek in the Transvaal gave one or two of our recruits the Transvaal bar !) and trekked along eastward, parallel to the river, thinking we had lost De Wet; but late in the afternoon we heard guns along the river, and went off at the gallop, just treading on De Wet's rear-guard as it crossed the Vaal with De Lisle on his heels. We could see his guns and wagons rounding a *kopje* towards Vredefort, and his rear guard was holding the *kopjes* overlooking the drift against De Lisle, when we came up on his flank.

As we galloped down to the same lot of *kopjes* they were on they gave it us pretty warm. We had to go through a wire fence where it had been cut, and the old mare was going very strong. I could as easily have held a train. Just as we got to the cutting in the fence a Martini bullet hit just in front of her, and splashed sand and stones in her face. She swerved off short, and just as I thought she was going smash into the fence she jumped it clean, to my astonishment. (It was sagging a bit from having been cut the other side.) Well, the Boers cleared after their convoy.

It was just getting dark now, and looked pretty uncomfortable, as it was coming over as black as a hat, and we could see there was going to be a bad storm, thunder and lightning going like it can go here. We were riding back to the column, at a walk, and one gun was having a few parting shots at the Boer convoy, when suddenly there was a blinding flash from the tail of the Joe wagons, and a roar that beat the thunder hollow—the last shell we fired had hit De Wet's ammunition wagon. By this time it was raining, and in five minutes was as dark as pitch; so we went up to where the wagon had been, and camped, making a fire out of the pieces of wagon. There were five Boer prisoners, and one of them said his brother had been driving the wagon; but it did not seem to worry him much.

I had to go on outpost down in the flat by a marshy stream, and myself and three men tied our horses to a telegraph pole and sat there all night. It rained as if it would never stop, thunder and lightning and wind. I was soaking wet through when I went in just at dawn. They had kept a fire up all night with the old wagon, and had already discovered some pieces of anatomy

CANADA

98

lying around. I had to go up the *kopje* to my section-sergeant, and about 120 yards from the explosion I came on a head and shoulders, just like a bust in marble—quite complete, except that the hair was singed off; and a little further on, a thigh.

After that we did not see anything of them for some time, and trekked round by Vredefort Weg down to Rhenoster and out towards Bothaville again. The day we got to Bothaville we got on their track again, and had some sniping; so made a long march, and got to Bothaville after dark. We had some shell fire about five miles out, and Le Gallais' horse was hit. We camped in the town: probably the Boers thought we had stayed five miles out.

No one slept much that night among the men, as we were all marching around the little town (which we had burnt) seeing what we could find. After everything was fixed up I went with my two mess-mates on a tour of inspection; this was about 11 p.m. The lancers who burnt the place had pretty well gutted it, but we found a huge sow which had taken up its residence in the bank! We murdered her with a very small pen-knife and proceeded to fresh fields. I struck a good house standing in its own ground, that had not been touched for some reason.

The veranda was full of boxes of crockery and small furniture, so I thought there might be something (eatable) inside, and was forcing a window in the most approved Sykes style when I heard a scuffle and a lot of swearing inside, and just as I cleared got a glimpse of several pyjama'd figures coming out of all the doors. The place must have been full of officers. I had no luck after that, so turned in about 2 a.m. in the main street.

We made an early start next morning, and my company was right flank guard. We crossed the drift over the Valsch and got out in our place. The convoy had hardly got over the *drift* when the advance guard was on the Boer camp! Of course we could not see, as there was a rise between, but this is what happened: The advance guard had barely got opened out properly when they topped a rise, and there were all the Boers' mules and horses grazing round and an outpost asleep about sixty yards in front of this *laager*, which was round a farmhouse with a dam.

The Boers' Kaffirs were the first to see ours, and they ran out to get the horses and mules in; and then our advance-guard opened fire point blank into the *laager*, which responded, all the Boers who could not get to their horses getting behind the dam wall. Each Joe as he got his horse or inspanned a Cape cart, cleared on his own to a line of scrub about three-quarters of a mile away, where presumably De Wet (who was the first to clear as usual) reformed them. Meanwhile we were coming along on the right flank, wondering what all the shell fire was about, for we never dreamt that they had been camped so close to us.

Suddenly we came over the rise just above the farm on the right, and were not left long in doubt as to what was going on when they saw us. Both sides were using case, but the Boers soon had to abandon their guns, and all got into the dam, or rather behind the dam-bank. At one time the rifle-fire was so hot that our guns were left, but about eight mounted infantry crawled up and got under them, so they were never really abandoned.

A man named Green, of the Lincolns, got the D.C.M. for carrying ammunition. He took a case along the firing line scarcely 100 yards from the position—a sufficiently plucky thing when you consider the effect a bullet would have in a case of ammuni-

BURMAH MOUNTED INFANTRY

tion; it would not be so bad, of course, with loose rounds. Early in the fight Le Gallais, Colonel Cross, and the staff, rode up to the farmhouse, which is almost on the dam, and going straight through looked out of a back window which overlooked the position. He was shot through the chest instantly, so was Colonel Cross, and I believe several others, till it came down to Major Welch's turn to command the column.

He was in charge of the convoy at the time, and on being sent for he came up at a comfortable hand-gallop, swinging his cane, and talking to himself, I've no doubt, as it was a great habit of his. He was proceeding to inspect the position, when he was shot through the neck. After this it was Tommy's battle—single men and little groups manoeuvring on their own.

A road runs past the farm with a shallow sandy bank, and they crawled up here, scooping little places for cover with their hands,, and every little salt bush had a man behind it. The pom-pom got up into the garden! and was worked and deserted for cover alternately, as the Boers' attention was attracted elsewhere.

At last some one of the Malta Mounted Infantry shouted "Fix bayonets!" and it was passed on. It is on record that just four men could fix bayonets, as the majority had been used for picqueting pegs so often that the socket was knocked flat! But the Boers did not know this, and stood up in a body waving anything white they had. Most of this we learnt after, as early in the fight the right flank guard was sent off to the right almost back to the river, where we were kept pretty busy by the men who had got away under De Wet, who were trying to get round our flank. They were round both sides, being opposed on the left by the dismounted men, and it might have ended differently if De Lisle had not come up, when they cleared, and we went back to the farm.

Unlike a good many well-known fights, Bothaville looked like a battle-field, dead horses everywhere. We passed Col. Cross's or Major Hickey's horse, a fine old English chap, standing in a pool of water, shot through, just in front of and just behind the flap of the saddle. Major Welch's horse was lying riddled about seventy paces from the *laager*. The guns looked chipped about, and the wagons and Cape carts were in splinters.

Every here and there little hollows had been scraped in the sand, most of them with blood marks in them. They were collecting the dead and wounded as we got there, in wagons, and they buried them, Boers and all. I don't know the numbers, but the percentage was biggest of wounded. There were 130 prisoners (some of the Staats Artillery) and six guns. Two of these were Q battery's, lost at Sanna's Post, and Q battery was with us at Bothaville. They were pretty glad to get their guns back, and all the wagons, etc.—a pretty good capture.

After we had buried the dead, and were sitting about while the hospital orderlies got the wounded fixed up in the farm, some of ours discovered two Boers lying in a little turf pigsty about thirty yards in front of the dam; one was dead, and the other shot through the whole length of his body. We got him out and made him comfortable; he was a bit surly, but said he was a Transvaal *burgher*, and that this lot of about 300 men, with all the guns, had only joined De Wet the day before. We put him in the farm, but he died shortly after.

We left Le Gallais, Major Welch, and all the serious cases in the farm, and struck out for Kroonstad, with prisoners, guns, etc., where we got quite a reception, and packed the captured guns in the market-square for a bit of bounce. We heard a day or two after of Le Gallais' and Tony Welch's death. Welch would have made a name for himself in the war if he had lived; he was the right man to command mounted troops. He was an amateur jockey at home, and cared more for horses than his drill. I remember once at Cork, on a General's inspection, they got the regiment into square, and Tony was told to get them back into column, which he had no idea how to do, apparently, for the adjutant coached him in a stage aside. We all thought we deserved a bar for Bothaville, but didn't get it.

Chapter 11

On the Basuto Border

We were in Kroonstadt now for ten days, which was the longest halt we had had since Bloemfontein. The mare got rid of me for the first (and only) time about a week after we came in. In a camp like that you get any amount of rations, and the horses are standing in forage all day and night, besides getting their 8 lb. of oats. The consequence was in a week my mare was as fat as butter again, and very full of herself. I was riding her down to water, bare-backed, when the string started trotting. . . I came about the third bound!

After about ten days we entrained and went off down south through Bloemfontein in coal trucks. We were already a pretty tough-looking crowd, and after the night in the coal dust we were pretty fit when we reached Bloemfontein, where we had to stay for a few hours to water the horses. Then on down to Edenburg, where we got an awful shock, as the first person we saw on the station was General MacDonald, and as we knew we were getting out we thought we were going under his command again. However, it turned out that he was in charge of communications down there and did not leave the line. I suppose we joined Pilcher here; if not, we were under Knox.

While we were camped at Edenburg we had one scare of Boers coming, for the town and all went out and galloped for a few miles, but saw nothing. Then off again through Reddersburg, and then to the right towards Wepener; and about here comes the next excitement. I was on right-flank guard. Mr. Jones was

Entrained for Edenburg

our officer (we had no captain). We were trekking through some fairly rough country—deep *dongas* and broken hills—and could not see the main body most of the time.

At one farm we struck all the ingredients for making powder in large quantities, so proceeded to destroy it, which took us some time, and we moved off at the gallop to make up the ground we had lost. Here we saw a Cape cart leave a farm in front and go like blazes straight to our front, parallel with the column. We pulled up to the farm and questioned the women, who were very excited, and would tell nothing but palpable lies. We knew De Wet was close, so we went after the Cape cart for all we knew (quite likely De Wet was in it).

We had a pretty long gallop, and Mr. Jones, myself, and two more were the only ones up, when we came over a rise and nearly ran into a herd of cattle being driven off from the *laager*, which we saw just to our left front, in the path of the column. We were within 500 yards of the whole outfit, and I tell you we lost no time in taking cover! They had got the alarm, and were packing up in the devil of a hurry. Their *laager* was at a farm under a *kopje*, and they must have been keeping very poor watch. Just as we were wondering what we had better do, our advance guard (good old "Binks" Murdoch in charge) opened fire from the *kopje* scarcely 300 yards from them; so they could not have had a post up there at all. We made a rush for it then to the *kopje*, and found the troops just arriving—tremendous excitement!- Mounted Infantry dismounting and doubling up the *kop* under a heavy rifle fire, as the Boers were making a stand while they got their guns, etc., away.

Just as we got there, two guns came up and started weighing in with shrapnel. The Malta Mounted Infantry started working round the foot of the hill, and we went up. It was warm going up; every now and then we had to lie down till they turned their attention elsewhere, till we got to a ledge where a lot of officers were lying, and some men too. Here they stopped us, and made us go one by one to the edge overlooking the camp. I thought it was rather rot till it came my turn; then I thought it was a good plan, and would have liked to have waited to see it was carried on properly, but someone in authority said "Go on over, Corporal!"

So I stood up and walked over to where Murdoch and the rest were lying. I say walked, but as soon as my head came over the skyline I doubled up and ran for it. There was a continual stream of bullets coming over like a machine gun, and when one just passed my ear it snapped, it was so close. There was a continual whizz and snapping, just like snapping your fingers, going on. I lay down on the edge and found myself looking over the camp, which was in tremendous confusion, inspanning Cape carts and wagons and Boers galloping about all over the place. We could not make out where all the good shooting came from, as all the Boers we could see were too busy to do much, and yet every time we raised an eyebrow they were chipping lumps off the *kopje* all round us.

There was a crowd of horses on the *kopje* about eighty yards below to our right front, and the men hidden among the rocks, but these we thought were the Malta Mounted Infantry, so we never took any notice of them till the camp was clear and the Boer convoy and cattle, etc., was filing off southward, when with a final withering fusillade (good expression!) these beauties made a rush for their horses and cleared like blazes!

We tried for a moment to kid ourselves that it was the Maltas going in pursuit; but we could see their clothes too plainly, and realised that we had been had again. They scattered at once, and we did some rapid firing at them, but only accounted for one of that lot that I know of. They drew off between two mountains to the south, and we went round to take stock. The machine gun was just on my right, so I strolled over there first and found the sergeant dead with a bullet through the brain, and one of the men hit in the arm.

Then down to where the Malta Mounted Infantry were (about fifty yards from where we thought they were; in fact, the officers had been using the revolver). There were about four hit here, and seven horses riddled. We then went down to the *laager*, and there were some Boers there—how many I don't know, I only saw the one myself.

After this we trekked south through Smithfield to Bethulie, and across the Orange into the Cape Colony. We used to hate working in the Colony, as we were not allowed to take anything; even firewood was bought and issued out. At Aliwal North we crossed into the Free State again, and camped just over the bridge. Aliwal North was all English, a pretty little place, and as we came through ladies and little girls, looking beautifully cool and clean, were all along the roadsides with trays of lemonade, milk, etc.

With a foolish (under the circumstances) return to "parade" no one was allowed to fall out, which made the people who had meant kindly look rather foolish. I noticed several poor little beggars of girls almost crying as troop after troop went by and none of them stopped for a drink. Then away up the Basuto border, supposed to be close on De Wet's heels, but we never came up with him till we got back to our old hunting grounds again between Thaba'nchu and Winburg, or rather, near Ficksburg, I think it must have been, but I'm a bit misled as to what happened for a few months at this time. However, I'll work the events in somehow, and if they are in the wrong order it won't matter.

We camped one night at Ficksburg—a pretty little place, all fruit trees—and next day we struck the trail again. A few of us were detached at a farm for some reason, and when we were catching up we came up with the machine gun section, and went with it. Just as we were passing a hill, all covered with bracken and furze, the Boers let drive and killed the gun mule, and there was a brisk little scrap for a few minutes. It is pretty rough country there and we soon lost them, but later on they made a bit of a stand, and the guns came into action; one officer of ours was killed on a *kopje*.[1]

1. After the fight we brought him down to the farm at the foot to bury him, and the brute of a woman made some remark like "Chuck him in the pigsty," or something of that sort. She was not treated civilly after that, and I shouldn't wonder if she is one of Emily Hobhouse's pet martyrs now.

I had been away from the company for some reason, and as I was riding up through the convoy to catch up, just as I passed the herd of cattle they drove along for meat, there was a terrific explosion, and a lyddite shell burst right amongst the butchers who were driving.

I thought it funny that I had never heard it coming, but it turned out that Findon, our company butcher, had picked up a live lyddite shell which our guns had fired, and after examining it had handed it over to his chum to see, and between them they dropped it! Findon's horse was nothing but a hide turned inside out; his legs were blown to bits almost, his chum and horse killed, two or three Kaffir drivers killed, and several bullocks! I just caught up the company as the Boers opened fire again from a line of *kopjes* behind a *donga*, and we raced for the *donga*, which was pretty close to the Boers, and got under cover, staying there till dusk.

I was holding horses in the bed of the *nullah*, and the Boers got a few men round each flank so that they could fire up and down the bed. I heard a flop, and one little mare fell down hit through the neck; however, she got up soon, and never seemed much the worse for it. Luckily it was just getting dark, for things were getting rather warm; and soon we retired to where the shell accident had happened, and camped. Findon was in the field hospital, and seemed to consider the affair rather a joke. It rained hard all that night; in fact, it usually did at this time.

Next morning my company was rear-guard, and the column trekked through a *nek* between two big round hills. One section of us held the hill on the right, and another the one on the left. I was in charge of the led horses on the right. For some reason they stopped up there till the column was out of sight, and I could hear them firing like blazes, and could tell they were getting it pretty hot by the bullets that came over the *kopje*.

Presently I saw the section on the left run down to their horses and clear at the gallop, so the Boers had that hill. It is nervous work holding horses in an engagement, as you don't know what is happening; and if the Boers get round the flanks, as they frequently do, it's bad for you—that is how our chaps were cut up later—and I was pretty glad to see our chaps come running down. I had the sergeant-major's horse, and as he took it he said, "We'll get it before we get away from here; they are coming round both flanks, and are nearly up to us on the *kopje!*"

So we all got mounted, and were only waiting for the officer whose horse I had. I don't know what he was doing, but it seemed ages before he appeared, strolling down as if he had a week. However, one Boer arrived at the top and took a shot at the other section that was out in the open—he never thought we were just under him. That made our officer run, and we opened out and "got"; but about a hundred yards or so back there was a running *spruit*, and we had to close in to the drift.

By this time a lot of Boers spotted us from the *kopje*, and made things hum as we crossed the drift. I was thinking how nice it would be if they shot my old mare and she fell on me in five feet of water. Just as we opened out the other side, one chap's horse did go down, and as the man scrambled clear the Boers concentrated their fire on him. I, of course, tried to pull up, but it's wonderful what a hard mouth a horse has on these occasions; if you'll believe me, I was almost out of range before I could even slacken pace(!). However, the chap mounted again and came on, so the horse was not hurt much.

We went for about two miles, and as the Boers were following us we took up another position, and got it pretty warm again, having to send in for reinforcements. Mr. Jones, our officer, had his horse shot. I think we must have had Christmas about now. I know we went north for a couple of days, and killed five Boers on a *kop* with shrapnel. After that I've lost count.

We spent that Christmas at a farm called Peru, and had hardly any water to drink. Then once, when we were near Senekal, there was a strong party of Boers reported to the north in some table-lands, so off we went after them. We had got into camp one evening when the outpost reported them coming our way; so we went out, and on topping a rise there they were all over the next rise, quite close. Neither side hardly fired a shot—we just stood and watched each other for a few minutes, then we went back to camp. That night, of course, we had a night march— thought we were going to do wonders. We came to a long, low table-land a bit before dawn, where they were supposed to be camped, and got up on top, then lay down till daylight.

Well, everything was right; when day broke they were there right enough at some Kaffir *kraals* at the edge of the kop; but, as usual, someone who was supposed to go round to cut off their retreat didn't go, or got lost or something, and our friends simply mounted and cleared. We got one prisoner! a most ceremonious old chap. As we took him down through the column he raised his hat and said "Good morning" to everyone individually.

CHAPTER 12

Chasing De Wet

I don't know the date, but I think about now must have been the De Wet hunt in the Colony; anyway, we'll work it in here! You must imagine us trekking south on De Wet's track, about a day's ride north of Thaba'nchu. We knew De Wet had a strong force and two or three guns—it was very funny the way we used to watch what guns old De Wet had. He was always our particular quarry. You might be riding along on his track not taking much interest in things.

After a fortnight's ride without seeing a Boer, you begin to think they are only inventions of the Uitlanders, when your right-hand man says, "Know what old So-and-so told me last night? De Wet called in at such-and-such a post and nabbed two guns! "Then you take interest in things again, and hope to goodness some other columns will work him till he loses those guns. I know I used to. This day we were riding with the convoy, and the main body in front struck the Boers early in the day. We could hear them firing. It was hilly country, and the main body of Boers must have let our advance go past them, as, on the convoy rounding a big green hill, there was the old "whom, whom" and a whiz, and two shells burst right among the leading wagons. That was one of the funniest sights I've seen.

Off the road it was cracked, ant-heapy broken ground, but the Kaffir drivers just turned short off and opened out and went across country for all their mules were worth—chattering, yelling, whistling! (When a Kaffir is astonished, he says "*hau*" and whistles.) We sat and laughed for about five minutes; but they soon sent back for us, and when we got up to the front it was a respectable engagement. Our chaps were taking a long line of hills that the Boers were on, all galloping up by companies. The Lincolns were going for the end of the spur on the right, us next, then Norfolks, Burmahs, 5th Mounted Infantry, etc.

I was sent with some message to the Lincolns, and when I came back our men were up the *kopje* and the horses at the foot. A private said to me, "You've got to take over these horses till the company comes down." Remembering the guns I made no objection to this, and sat down listening to the spare bullets coming over. They were getting it pretty warm on top! Soon a man of the Lincolns came down hit through the neck and stomach, so I went off to look for a doctor. I found one at a farm which they had as hospital. The officer commanding the Burmah Mounted Infantry was here shot in an unmentionable spot! and there were several more casualties. But I got an old Yeomanry doctor to come with me, and left him with the wounded man. Soon there were a good many coming down hit—mostly of the Lincolns, as they got a cross fire.

One of them was killed. He gave me rather a shock, poor chap! I went round to their horses to see how they were getting on, and the first man I came to was lying on his back with a handkerchief over his face. I thought he was asleep till he didn't answer me. Towards dusk they sent down to warn me for outpost with fifteen men. I said it was not my turn—nor was it, as I had been on stable guard (horse-lines) the night before. But I'd have given something an hour later to have said nothing and gone.

The next corporal for duty was a man named Sales, a very handsome chap and a quiet, decent fellow, too. He was up on the *kopje*, but things were quieter up there by now, and they told him to come down to get his men together. He turned and started to crawl back, when a lance-corporal (poor old "Billy" Paine—he died of dysentery afterwards because he would not go to hospital for fear of losing his pony that he had got fond of) called to him chaffingly to stand up, as they could never hit him!

Sales laughed and stood up, and had not taken a stride before they had him—through the right arm, in at the arm-pit, through his body, and the bullet lodged in his left arm, breaking it! When they got to him he said he thought he was hit in the legs! The bullet must have touched the spine. I helped carry him down to the ambulance, and the only thing he seemed to feel was the broken arm. That left me the last corporal of the old lot that had started out from Bloemfontein.

We slept at the foot of the *kopje* that night, and joined the main body in the morning. We had lost pretty heavily, chiefly among the Burmah Mounted Infantry, who had several officers killed and wounded and a lot of men. There were two killed and five or six wounded on our little *kopje*. An artilleryman did something good here: his gun was getting captured, and he worked it till they were right on him, and then broke something that made it useless, or something of that sort. That was Tabac'sberg.

Next day I was riding Sale's horse, as it was a good one. We were on advance-guard, my section on the left. I went up the convoy before we got out and saw Sales in the ambulance. He was not in pain, but I think he knew it was all up with him, poor chap! We were coming along over a great flat stretch of *veldt* about midway, with Thaba'nchu showing blue in the distance and some very rough country between us and it, and a grassy knoll just on our front. We had been watching some black specks on this for miles, and when we got nearer we made out one Kaffir and a flock of sheep, so we thought it was all right; but when we got about 150 yards from the top, five mounted men suddenly appeared on the crest and let us have their magazines full.

We were opened out, of course, we and started to gallop round the left flank of the rise, which took us out of sight of the column. There were only four of us, as it was the extreme left of the screen. They gave it us pretty warm while we were getting round—one horse was hit; but as soon as they saw we were getting round they cleared out, and when we got round we had a turn at them. We didn't take much notice of them when we had a look about, for there was the whole of the mob getting away from a farm under a *kopje*, and about thirty coming our way at the gallop—to cover the retreat, no doubt!

We got back to the top of the rise pretty quick, till we could see the column; and then we saw that they were watching too, and though the guns were up and everything, and we only had to gallop down to get at least all their convoy, we stayed there and watched them trek off to Thaba'nchu. We were wild.

There was a line of block-houses from Bloemfontein to Ladybrand, but we knew De Wet could break through them when he liked. (De Wet is very cock-a-whoop in his book about always being able to get through a line of block-houses. I don't see that there was much difficulty in it, especially at night-you simply had to run the gauntlet of about twelve men's fire, whereas in an engagement or skirmish you'd generally have to run chances with fifty or sixty firing at you. I don't believe, myself, that Kitchener ever meant to stop Boers with them.

They were an excellent way of breaking the country up so that you always knew where a big body of men were.) It seems that our column commander did not want to take his convoy, for that was the only means of holding the Boers in a body till you could capture the lot, and we were not strong enough for that. We followed them up slowly, and De Wet broke through the block-house line that night. It happened just where some of my company details from Bloemfontein were posted. They told us about it afterwards. The man that told me said he was down in the creek getting water about dusk, when suddenly about sixty Boers appeared at the gallop. He hid in the reeds and watched them.

They galloped up to the nearest cover to the block-house and opened a murderous fire. A couple of them under cover of this went and cut the wire fence that joins each block-house, and after dark De Wet and the main body drove straight through. It was simple enough. They were shouting out to our men that they would come back for them presently! Of course they could not harm our fellows in the house; but they couldn't come out, and they made it very unpleasant for them to shoot through the loopholes. Joe used to use shot guns when he was block-house running; and shooting at a loophole with buck shot, some pellets were sure to go in and hit the man inside in the face!

De Wet trekked off down to Rouxville or that way, and we went in to Bloemfontein and trained down to Bethulie. Here Capt. Leigh joined us, bringing a strong draft from the Regiment, and he brought the news of Corporal Sale's death. He died as soon as he got in to Bloemfontein—bad luck for his people, for he had had his brother, a sergeant in some Dragoons, killed down Ladysmith way.

Now, of course, we were in front of De Wet again, as it would take him some days to trek down, and we made a short detour to the west of the line to see if any had got down that way. (This was the line from Springfontein to Port Elizabeth—not the Cape Town Line.) We crossed again just below the junction and met the Boers directly, but only got some big gun practice.

That night, I remember, it rained cats and dogs, and everyone had turned in pretty early, when, about 9 p.m., they shouted, "Turn up for your rum!" The only man who was not under the blankets was my old mate Pile, an old Hampshire carter—a regular tough old card. He went and got the rum, a canteenfull, for the section; then he came back and called out to the men to

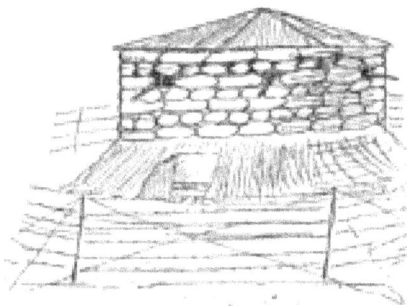

A SANDBAG BLOCKHOUSE

turn up for theirs, taking care not to call too loud. No one came, so he presumed no one wanted any; he gave me a good swig and I went to sleep.

Next morning we made an early start, and it was still raining, and the only happy man there was old Pile! He didn't care how things went. Lost his saddlery—when he found it, could not get it on the horse, laughing all the time; altogether he was pretty wet. The sergeant-major spotted him and told me to see that he did not start with the company, so I stayed after the company had gone on and got him mounted, and the last I saw of him he was singing rollicking songs with the convoy, much to the delight of the Kaffir drivers.

We passed a place where someone had had a brush with our friends; there were a lot of dead horses and a tent standing deserted. Then we crossed the line again at Springfontein and struck down through Phillipopolis to the Orange. De Wet had just crossed in front of us. We had to swim part of the way over as the Orange was in flood, and there was a tremendous business getting the convoy over, a lot of mules being drowned.

At last they outspanned all the mules and fetched back the gun horses in teams, four horses to a wagon, and they got them over all right. It was fine to see them humping themselves going up the steep road out of the river bed: I expect it reminded the old chaps of a full 'bus up Ludgate Hill! This was somewhere near Stormberg, I believe. It was rotten country for about five miles from the river—great mountains and *krantzes*—but it cleared a bit when we got to Phillipstown, where Plumer had had a brush with De Wet that day! We only stopped there about an hour, I think, as we were hot on the trail, and then left for the line between Orange River and De Aar.

About half-way to camp my old mare, in very different condition to what she had been months back at Kroonstad when I drew her, gave out in the same way as my first horse—she also had lasted longer than the majority—and next day I had to ride on a bullock wagon, while the mounted troops went on as hard as they could lick, expecting to catch De Wet before he reached the line. I was rather sick at being out of it.

We did not reach the line till about 4 a.m. next morning, and it was a strange sight when we did. The troops had got at some cases of rum in the station, which proved of more interest than De Wet. I won't go into details, but Hontkraal was always known afterwards in the column as "Rumfontein"! It was no one's fault but Tommy's (unless it was the fault of the quarter-guard on the station), as no one in authority knew anything about it till the mischief was done. But Pilcher never forgave the column, and drunk or sober we trekked that morning.

One of our men on left flank guard had a sleep on the way and got lost for three days. I say we trekked, but I was left with about eight men drawing remounts. I got a North American. He was a good horse, but very lame. However, as he used to go at an ambling canter you didn't feel it much. The worst part about him was that he used to fall without any warning; if he could manage it, always on a hard road when the regiment was trotting in sub-sections, and he was well up in front, so that a few hundred men could ride over me! We caught up the column that night riding over Sandy Karroo—about the most god-forsaken country I've struck—and we got the news then about those dragoons being captured and the officer's retaliating on De Wet for striking him.

We were close on De Wet when he was stuck in that bog. Pretty well due west we went, passing south of Hopetown, getting news of De Wet all the way—in fact, striking most of his camp. We and Plumer were the closest up all through in this hunt. We were well on the scent till we got to a river—Salt River, I think. It was on the way to Prieska when we got to one drift, and Plumer to the next, and we thought we had passed De Wet as there was no sign of his having crossed at either, and he could not have crossed anywhere else; so we both struck back, beating for him.

It turned out afterwards that he had laid in the river bank between us and Plumer, on the same side as us, and when we came back he came back after us keeping behind!!—bad scouting on someone's part.[1] We had absolutely no forage for our horses at this time, and the way we kept them alive was this: all the troops slept out in a big ring round the camp, and let all the horses loose inside all night. Even there there was no grass, only salt bush, which most of them would not eat. We lost a lot of horses on that trek, but no one got much fighting, I think, though, the author of *On the heels of De Wet* has made a very interesting little book about it.

As far as I can make out his column was seldom within twenty miles of De Wet! We all concentrated in Hopetown, and the night we got there a strong patrol from all the columns went out and gathered up about forty prisoners of Hasbruck's commando as they were trying to cross the Orange. They were in a wretched state, no horses and hardly any clothes. The excitement seemed to be over now. We stayed a couple of days in Hopetown, then sauntered into Orange River station and stayed a day or so there, getting a nice swim in the Orange (not before I wanted a bath!).

We suddenly seemed to wake up one day and shot off over Orange River bridge and north-east towards Bloemfontein, past Ramah and Ram-dam. (This was the country over which the 7th Mounted Infantry had made the first march of their existence two years or so before!) We hoped we were going to Kimberley, but were disappointed. About half-way between Orange River and Bloemfontein we struck them again. (I don't know whether this was De Wet or not; probably it was Hertzog, or Nieuhondt; anyway, they were pretty strong.)

We didn't get any heavy fighting, but just nasty little nerve-shaking "incidents." For instance, one day the 5th Mounted Infantry were away on the right, and they got a prisoner. They sent him in with one man. (I don't know why they didn't send two.) On the way in they came to a farm with another Boer there, and the Mounted Infantry man held him up all right; but on taking his rifle and bandolier he stupidly took both hands to put it on his own shoulders, on which the two Joes manned him and

---

1. I know whose, but won't give it away (it was not me).

strangled him—at least, that is how we got the yarn, though I don't see how they knew what happened, unless they captured the Boers or unless some Kaffir saw it.

Then again, a 5th Mounted Infantry man was up in an orange tree at a farm under a *kopje*, and they shot him from the top of the kop. Next time it was my company that figured. We were on advance-guard, and at the mid-day halt we had got to a great basin, the column having halted under the *kopjes* at one side, whilst we were nearly across the basin facing the *kopjes* that formed the rim of the other side, as it were. The road went through a *nek* in front of us. We knew there were a lot of Boers the other side of these *kopjes*, for they had been in front all day; so Capt. Leigh sent a lance-corporal and three men on to be observation post on the road where it went over the *kopje*, meaning them, of course, to keep in sight of us.

Old Pile, my mess-mate, was one of the three men. I remember I was carrying our rations that day, and laughed at him as he was going off, for he could get nothing to eat without me. He used to ride a great gaunt raw-boned animal that he had had for a long time and had got quite fond of; he called it "Charlie," and would never get a remount.

After they had gone an orderly came out to us to say we could join the column, as they were going to camp there for the night, so off we went. The lookout post ought to have kept

"Jim" Pile on "Charlie"

in sight of us, as then they would have come in when we did, and that's what we expected they would do. I remember that the sergeant-major (Weston), Sergeant Murdoch, my section sergeant, and myself were riding with Captain Leigh, and he was telling us a great yarn of a column he had seen somewhere before he joined us (he had not been long out from India). He said, as soon as they got to camp, they had all stripped their shirts off and started searching for lice. "Most extraordinary sight" he said! We three looked at each other with a sickly smile! We'd all been there many a time!

We had not been in camp long when a man of the 5th Mounted Infantry came along to our camp at the gallop. I suppose he had been foraging on his own in front, for he said: "Those four men of yours are getting it pretty tight out there." The captain took half the company out to investigate, and this is what had happened:

When they got to the top of the hill they saw a conical *kopje* about a quarter of a mile in front, which looked a good place for a lookout. They didn't worry about not seeing us; they made sure we were coming on in half an hour or so, so down they went. They left one man (I forget his name—they used to call him "Rags" in the company for obvious reasons) with the four horses at the bottom, and the lance-corporal and Pile and the other man Russell started off up.

Well, the Boers must have been watching them all the time, for they had not got twenty yards up when about twenty of them came round each side of the kop at an easy hand-gallop. "Rags "thought things looked bad, so let a yell to warn the others; and seeing it was useless waiting, let go the three horses and made a spirited break for camp. He didn't get there till after the man who warned us, though. He got free with a clean gash of a mauser bullet right across his back (Gamblin was his name).

The Boers thought the other three were "a chuck in "for them, but they reckoned without Russell, who practically took charge (he was a reserve man), as the Lance-Jack was only a youngster. At the first volley they were all hit (they were scarcely twenty paces off). Pile's arm was broken, the corporal hit in the thigh with buckshot, and Russell in the hand.

Pile, with admirable generalship, promptly fell down and pretended to be dead!! and they took no more notice of him. Russell got the lance-corporal to the top of the *kop* and held off the foes for a bit; then while they were manoeuvring to get round him, he got the corporal along a ridge that joined the *kopje* to the rest of the hills, and when he was relieved was a mile away from the place. A good many V.C.'s have been easier earned. I daresay old Pile would have obliged with a few bars of the "Cock o'the North" if he had not been kidding himself he was dead!

We got them all in. Poor old Pile was invalided home, but all the others came back to duty in time. Russell had a grand little pony, and that and the Corporal's were taken, but when we trekked out past that *kopje* next day there was old "Charlie "grazing about as happy as possible without saddle or bridle. Joe had no use for a camel; and there was a laugh right through the column when we saw him. Pile was a character, and he and "Charlie" were well known. When they told Pile he smiled and said, "Ah, they don' know a good horse when they see un."

Nothing further happened till we got to Bloemfontein, where we stayed a few days and did not enjoy ourselves much, as Pilcher kept us on fatigue all the time by way of getting even with us for the Hontkraal affair.

CHAPTER 13

Clearing the Farms

After leaving Bloemfontein we went out east of the line again and started clearing the farms. The column used to camp in a central place, generally on a plain with *krantzes* all round the skyline, and at the foot of the *krantz* there were always farms (about the best I've seen out here were round that district; and they had any amount of stuff, corn, etc., and stock too, besides beautiful fruit—mostly oranges and peaches).

The column would halt for a week or so and send out patrols of one company to each farm to bring in the women and destroy the provisions. The first day my company went out on our own to a farm under a huge *krantz*, taking mule wagons with us to fetch *mealies* away in and the women, etc. We thought the country was pretty clear, so did not take many precautions, going up to the farm more or less in a body. The farm was clear, but there were a dozen or so Boers on the top of the *krantz*

(which was a table-land), and they let a volley into us which killed one of the wagon mules, so we attacked the *kopje*. They did not wait for us, but cleared down a goat track the other side. After that we always took the *kopje* first.

One day the column was going to shift camp, and two or three companies of us went on in front early. We came to a big plain closed in on all sides by hills and rough country, and I was sent off to call in two men of the flank-guard who had gone to a farm in the hills which was not safe, as we knew the hills were full of Boers. When I came back the company was engaged at pretty close quarters, and soon after had to retire to a small *kopje* out in the open. As we were galloping across the open a fellow of the Norfolks, who was riding a little to my left, made a dive over his horse's shoulder, and when we were at the *kopje* (I was down below in charge of led horses) the adjutant brought him in. He was hit clean through the heart.

We were held up then till the column came along, so we buried him down by a dam. We took one prisoner, a nasty looking customer, riding with only a blanket for a saddle, and no boots.

Our next adventure was clearing a farm again. Only our company and the Lincolns were on it, and we had to go out about five miles to a place called Clocolan, where there was a store and blacksmith's shop. The Boers were in the riverbed just by, but we soon drove them out; and my section (Sergeant Murdoch) was on lookout post in front, while they chucked all the *mealies*, etc., into the river. (This was supposed, of course, to be destroying the Boers' food supply, which was impossible as long

OUR PRISONER

123

as there were Kaffirs in the country). When this was finished we had to go on and clear two farms under a great *krantz*. We knew we should catch it here, as the Boers were watching us from the top of the *krantz*.

On the way up, the section on our right foolishly rode close past a Kaffir *kraal* where there happened to be a few Joes. We had to cover their retreat, and we were not bored for half an hour or so. We got in a watercourse. I was holding horses and I had no cover, for I could not get the horses anywhere where there was any. The firing-line were all right, as they were in the ditch. After a time I sent up to tell Murdoch if he didn't come away he'd have to walk, as I was going, so he came. He wanted to know what was up till he got exposed himself, then we cleared pretty quick. One little cockney was in such a hurry that he tried to jump a wet *donga*, and went in, horse and all!

There was some pretty hot firing round the two farms by this time, and our chaps got driven back. We collected in a dry *donga* almost out of range, and I was hoping they were going to give it up, or wait for reinforcements!

While we were in this *donga* I noticed a man on foot come from one of the farms from which ours had been driven back, and start running down the line of a fence with stone posts towards us, under a heavy fire from the *kopje*. We were rather enjoying the sight, and betting was quite brisk, every yard he made heightening the odds on our man, when suddenly a mounted Boer rounded the foot of the *krantz* and came at an easy hand canter down the road which was bordered by the fence.

This, of course, was serious, for we guessed that our man had not handicapped himself with a rifle for a 1,700 yards' sprint! and Joe would probably not trouble to take him prisoner. This proved to be the case, for when he was about 300 yards behind, Joe dismounted and took a steady snap at our man. We thought he had him, but Tommy was up to him, and just before he fired dived behind one of the stone posts, and before Joe realised he had missed was making even time for the next post!

By this time three of ours (probably men who had betted on

the running man) were mounting to go out to the rescue, and after carefully assuring myself that there was only one Boer, I resolved to join the expedition! As we galloped up at about ten paces interval (like a sub-section tent pegging) Joe had another couple of shots at Tommy, who repeated his tactics successfully. I took care that the man next to me should be the one to rescue the man, as I reflected that Joe would not shoot at me if he had two men to shoot at ten yards off; and this consideration had weight, for he was now only about 120 yards off, and had taken cover behind a hump.

The man who reached the fugitive was a Corporal White, and he stupidly dismounted and began an *indaba* with the other; but almost immediately he mounted again, and cantered off back to the *donga*! This, you will observe, upset my comfortable arrangements, for I was next man, and friend Joe was carrying on with the snapping with a regularity that would have brought him much credit in a "continue the practice" exercise at home.

However, something had to be done, so I jogged the old Argentine's mouth and ranged alongside the man who had started to run again. I kicked one foot out of the stirrup and told him if he couldn't get up behind me before I counted three he could keep on running, as I wasn't going to wait. He did it in rather under the time, I should think, but Joe got in a shot that regularly twanged past our ears like a banjo; then we broke for the *donga*, the old Argentine grunting like an escape of gas every time the double weight came down!

I had the comfortable knowledge that if I was shot the man who was the cause would have to be shot first. He was one of the Lincolns, whose horse had been shot at the farm, and he had waited thinking we were coming back, but we had been so long that he got scared and resolved to chance it. He told me, when he got his breath, that White had gone back because he was hit through the stomach. They sent him in to Bloemfontein, but he died six weeks after.

Soon after I got back we all formed up and charged the *krantz*, galloping up to the foot and climbing up. We were so puffed when we got to the top that a few Boers could have walked along and knocked us over with a stick; but they cleared as soon as they saw we meant coming, our only casualties being one man hit through the shoulder.

Of course, we lived like lords all this time, turkeys, geese, sucking-pigs, chicken, etc., being so plentiful that we used to eat our ration bully sometimes for a change! Besides this, we got any amount of milk, butter, honey and so on at the farms, the only thing we seldom got being bread. One day we went on patrol to the Basuto border on the Caledon river, and at a farm just on the banks the old Boer was sitting on the Basuto bank conversing in shouts with his *frou* on our side. We could not capture him, I suppose, over the border—anyway, we only laughed at him, and did not try—but in the great brick oven we found a tremendous batch of bread just done. It ran about three loaves each, so the old lady must have been cooking for a commando.

At Senekal we had a little adventure. We were camped just outside the town—a little dopper place of the usual type stuck down in the *veldt*; a square with the ugly Dutch church in the middle, and the principal stores round and a few streets or lanes running from it in parallel lines till they suddenly stop at open *veldt*, and the usual *kopje* hanging over it. My mess-mate Guyatt, the shoeing smith, was a great cook, and this night he had surpassed himself by making a beef-steak pudding in a Kaffir three-legged pot.

It was about 9 p.m., everyone else was asleep, and we were waiting for the pudding to be cooked, when a wretched orderly-sergeant or someone came along the lines shouting "Saddle up! March in half-an-hour! "Another night march! Pilcher was a beggar for night marches and early starts; his orders generally read, "reveille at 3, march at 4"!

Well, when we were saddled up and ready, our pudding was barely boiled. However, Guyatt seized the Kaffir pot and we started off at the trot through the town, Guyatt getting black all over, and his horse dancing about every time the hot pot touched his withers. Luckily, at the other side of the town, they halted

SANCTUARY

for a few minutes to get together in the dark, and we bolted our pudding, throwing away the pot! Then we started off on the old game that we were getting thoroughly sick of, sleepy and cold, tramping along all night with an occasional short trot.

We used to have long sleeps as we were riding along, and you did get sleepy when perhaps you were doing a night march one night, outpost the next, and another night march the next! As I was saying, we used to go to sleep mounted, and only wake up when we had got such a swing on with nodding that we'd find ourselves just diving over the horses' shoulders!

This time I was just getting an unusually heavy sleep, owing probably to the beef-steak pudding, and we were riding along a road in a body—we had to, night-marching, otherwise we could never have kept together—when I was wakened suddenly by a violent report in my ear, as it seemed. As I gathered myself together I saw that we were approaching two low *kopjes*, one at either side of the road, about eighty yards in front of us; and as I was wondering what had happened, there was a regular fusillade from each of these, and notwithstanding the darkness some of the shot were hitting amongst us.

We were so taken by surprise that we were edging off different ways, for we had got so into the habit of opening out under fire. We were all mixed up, as you do get on a night march, for if you go to sleep and your horse is a fast walker, he draws ahead till he gets to the head of the column, and no one knows who

you are or cares, so you wake up in a different regiment!

This time I was up with the Norfolks or someone, and we were all fidgeting about, not knowing whether to do a bunk or not (if we had, half of us would never have found camp again), when Major Lloyd of the Norfolks, who was in command, shouted "charge" as if it were Balaclava; and we all let a yell and went for the two *kopjes* in a mob as hard as we could gallop. I never laughed so much in my life. There were great stones and cracks in the earth, and chaps were going head over heels about every ten yards, swearing like blazes. I found myself going for the *kop* on the right, and we galloped straight up it, stones or no stones.

I was riding the old lame North American broncho animal, and he went as if he was born to it, hitting sparks off the rocks with his nose at every jump. They ceased fire when we got about half-way up, and when we got to the top we could just see a few of them clearing out. We ought to have stopped, of course, but the chaps were excited and went after them. I went after what I thought was a Cape cart, but lost it. We didn't get together again till daylight. It seems, they were five miles nearer us than we had thought.

When I found my section, Guyatt told me that when the charge went off he and Sergeant Murdoch galloped straight along the road (the most sensible thing to do) and came round on the Boers just as we drove them off the top. He attached himself to an old Boer, who went off down the road as hard as he could lick. Guyatt was shouting "hands up" with his rifle slung (I believe none of us had unslung our rifles, I know I hadn't), and going like blazes after him, when the old chap jinked like a pig and went off at a tangent, and Guyatt went over the edge of

a six-foot sandy *sluit*, distinctly hearing (he swears) the old Joe chuckle as he fell. When his horse had done rolling on him, of course the old man was well away.

Then we went up to Reitz, and hearing that Steyne, etc., were there, Pilcher got up a night attack, and we rode in and held some houses round the outskirts of the town till daybreak. The guides swore it was all right and the Boers were there still; but in the morning, of course, the place was empty, so we burnt it by way of getting our own back, or rather, practically burnt it, as every column in Africa seems to have burnt Reitz at some time or other.

Then one day we found ourselves at Ventersburg Road station again (it was here that my first horse gave out, you know), and a brand new yeomanry crowd came up the line to join us. I was on the platform trying to buy groceries at the refreshment room when they arrived, and they were asking us if they were likely to see any active service, and whether there were many Boers round there.

As I had heard that we were going out Bothaville way again, I was able to assure them that they were not too late. The first day out five of them got captured and were sent in stripped, with a note from Nel, I think it was, to say that the equipment was pretty good on the whole, but the horses were not up to his standard; and would Pilcher give them better ones next time they went out, as he was rather short of horses! We had to find one man per section to go and show them how to cook, etc., and a corporal of ours, named Tilbury, went as sergeant-major.

That night a lot of horse-stealing was done. Men from the column with bad horses took them over to the yeomanry lines, and while one engaged the sentry on horse- lines in conversation the other went and took a good horse off the line, putting his own old crock in its place.

CHAPTER 14

A Rear-Guard Action and a New Mount

We trekked out west of the line, after this, where the Boers were gathered pretty thick all along the Valsch River. Two or three yeomanry used to get captured every time they went out on flank-guard, or anything, and Pilcher got rather wild with them. They used to load up their horses fearfully, too; carry everything they could pile up. One day Pilcher rode along and dismounted every man who had too much, and handed over a lot of their horses to us.

However, they were just out from London, and bucked up a lot afterwards. Rather a contrast between this chap's equipment (in my sketch) and that of the Boer (earlier sketch)! Of course,

OVERLOADED

before he was captured, he had a rifle and *bandolier*. Otherwise, a pocket full of dried tobacco leaves was *all the field equipment he could find*, to quote Kipling. It was foolishness, too, for if it had been insisted upon, every man of ours could have been quite as mobile in a week as the Boers were. It is only a matter of custom whether you sleep warm in a big coat, or five or six blankets. For long periods we had nothing but the sweaty saddle blanket.

That was at the time when there were white frosts, too, and we got used to it in a few days; anyway, we hardly ever carried anything on the saddle after the first month or two.

After we had trekked round a bit one day I thought the country looked familiar, and suddenly we came out of a belt of scrub right on to the Bothaville farmhouse, where the fight was. All the graves had been railed in and everything was quiet enough now. Young Coulson, our adjutant, rode over and had a look at Tony Welch's grave—they had been very good friends. Poor chap! he was buried beside Welch within the week.

We went along the south bank of the Valsch, westward, seeing signs that the Boers were pretty thick everywhere; in fact, their *vedettes* were hovering about on the north side all the time, occasionally coming down to the bank for a snipe at us. When we got to Hauptman's Drift the column halted, and the 7th Mounted Infantry and a pom-pom were sent on about twelve miles to another *drift*—Commando Drift, I think. We got there all right, and found a farm with any amount of pumpkins and potatoes, so did ourselves pretty well.

Next morning, our outposts were firing pretty heavily all round, and Lloyd reinforced them; but about 10 a.m. a patrol of Burmah Mounted Infantry came from the column to tell us that they had had a night attack and were going back towards Bothaville, and we were to follow! This was pleasant for us, as we should have to camp that night somewhere near where the whole column had been attacked the night before!

However, we packed up and tracked off for Hauptman's Drift. We captured a pretty big head of cattle on the way, and reached the drift about 4 p.m. I was on lookout post on the drift while they halted for a time, and I did not like the look of things at all, as there were any amount of Boers the other side of the river, and messengers going off in different directions at the gallop, evidently to get more!

We moved off then straight away from the river at right angles to our previous route, and about dusk came to a ruined farm in a hollow that ran away down to the river, with an old broken dam and a cattle *kraal*. We put the cattle in the *kraal* and posted outposts of a corporal and three men at each corner of the little camp about 200 yards out, the camp being just close to the cattle *kraal* and about eighty yards from the dam.

Our two Dutch guides seemed to be in a bit of a stew and got leave to sleep in the farmhouse, so we expected something was up. However, we picketed the horses and got our fires ready, and about 8.30 I went up to draw the section's meat. A man of the K.O.S.B. had come over to our fire—to boil his canteen as he had no wood.

As I was coming back from the wagon with the meat on my head there was a bang, and a bullet whistled through a lighted tent close by. I had been expecting something of the sort, so before the volley that followed I had dropped the meat in the horse-lines and made a buck-leap up the lines for my saddle, where my rifle was. I noticed then the chap of the K.O.S.B. lying almost on the fire he had been shot dead by almost the first shot.

Without orders every fire and light went out in camp. (With unpardonable want of forethought, Guyatt emptied a beautiful chicken stew we had on our fire.) Then we all grabbed our guns and ran out on the flanks, just as an enraged roar reached us from Captain Leigh's tent, where a bullet had smashed a lot of the crockery on the table. I thought for a minute that they had got us, as we could see they were inside the outpost line; but after about ten minutes' heavy firing on both sides they slackened off and cleared, followed by derisive jeers from Tommy

They had had the best of it, though, for they had shot three men, any amount of horses, and stampeded several lines of horses. (Major Lloyd lost five that got away with their picqueting ropes and pegs.) Besides this, they took the cattle out of the *kraal*, under cover of the firing and general confusion, and shot a Kaffir who was sleeping by the *kraal*. We slept out on the flanks all night. Next morning we saw that they had been behind the old dam-bank not eighty yards away.

We did not make a start till after 8 a.m., as we had to bury the dead and collect what horses were in sight that had stampeded; but at last we moved off. (All the outpost came in all right; the one that was outside the Boers during the firing had had a fire in a little hollow, and the sentry spent the ten minutes or so of the engagement sitting on it! They were not anxious to attract attention.)

We left an observation post on the far side of the camp on a rise when we moved off, and the usual fatigue party to clean up camp, pick up dropped ammunition, etc., and my company went off with the little convoy of five or six wagons and a couple of Cape carts or so; the K.O.S.B. were rearguard. When we had gone nearly a mile we heard firing behind, and Major Lloyd and young Coulson, the Adjutant, cantered back. Then an orderly came flying up to us and we went back at the gallop to the rear-guard; and it was a mix up. The K.O.S.B. were all dismounted and spread out on either side of the road, with Boers by the hundred scarcely a hundred yards from them, while odd men of ours from the look-out post and camp fatigue were coming up with and through the Boers!

The pom-pom and machine-gun were on the road, and every now and then the Joes would rush them and get right up to them; but the rear-guard (the whole regiment nearly was rear-guard by now) made it too hot for them. The reason that they could get so close was that the ground lay in great ridge and furrow, like a pasture at home, so that as soon as we mounted and galloped from one ridge to the next the Boers were galloping up the hill just behind us.

We got in with the K.O.S.B.'s just on the right of the road, and I was holding horses (which meant in this case that I stood with four horses a yard or so behind the firing-line, who lay or knelt down to fire). The horse next me on my left got his eye blown out, and the one on the right got his saddle all ripped about by a ricochet, so I was feeling happy. I tried to persuade Sergeant-Major Weston that it would be better for each man to hold his own horse, so that everyone could fire, but he was not having any!

We had to leave our wounded where they were hit, some dozen getting left; only one of ours got away, and he was hit mounted, so rode straight after the wagons; but we could see the Boers going over, too, which was not often the case. One very determined chap on a grey pony kept leading rushes for the pom-pom, and at last, as he was trying again—he got about thirty yards from us, coming up the road like smoke—someone got him, and he went over his pony's withers straight on his head. Captain Leigh was in charge by the pom-pom, and they say if it had not been for him they would have had it. I know it was a close thing several times.

Once they got up as far as the last wagon! One of our side was hit in the arm and body, and it made us wild to see a Boer come up and make him "hands up" with his arm hanging over from the break! Then a Cape cart dropped behind with one horse dead and the other hit, and the driver, an officer's servant, sitting up straight in the cart. We shouted to him to come on, but he never moved, and we found afterwards that he was dead, too. This was on a rise with a bigger hollow than usual between it and the next one we took up, and we got back on the Boers all right for him, as the pom-pom got the range on the Cape cart (about 300 yards) and waited.

As we expected, the Boers all crowded round the cart, and then they gave them the whole belt full. Men they captured, whose horses had been shot, said there were about eight down round the cart!

Just here we got helio communication with the main column, and we were not sorry! The Boers saw it, too, and came no further; so we left notes for them on the bushes, mostly insulting. (This was exactly a year to the day, from the rear-guard action out of Lindley with Ian Hamilton, and we asked if any of them remembered it.) I suppose they had driven us about six miles—I know it seemed a long time! Several miserable-looking objects left the Boers and came over to us, who turned out to be the prisoners whose horses were shot, stripped naked bar the shirt! They said they saw a lot of Boers down along the road, and brought us news of some of our wounded.

The ambulance went out after we joined the column, and brought in the wounded and dead or rather, buried the dead in the little cemetery of the Bothaville fight. Coulson got the D.S.O. or V.C. or something—at least, his people got it, as he was dead. It appears that when he went back past us he found the machine gun getting it very warm in the old camp, and he went to them.

In getting away one of them had his horse hit and could not get him along, as he had no spurs; seeing which, Coulson changed horses with him, and the horse dropping, got left. However, another man went back and got Coulson up behind him; but his horse was shot, too, and the man, seeing Coulson lying senseless, thought he was dead (as he may have been), and came away. Coulson's body was found in a *mealie* patch some paces off, which looks as if he had come round and crawled there for cover.

As the lookout post that we left came through the camp the Boers were in it, having come up the gully at the gallop between them and the main body. Our chaps did not think they were Boers at first, till a fellow called Fraser said, "Well, Boers or not, here goes for that old ——" and shot one dead, which opened the ball, of course.

After this we went in to the line and down to Brandfort. I still had the old lame animal that I drew at the time of the big drink at Hontkraal, but I had had him blistered and cured his lameness, but could not cure him of falling down at most unexpected times. Now, however, his time was up, and he was getting very shaky. He had lasted very well—in fact, considering

II.

I

his lameness, very well indeed—but at Brandfort there was a big lot of remounts coming up the line for us, so I reported the old fellow as unfit for further duty, and got him cast. The only thing about him that I regretted was a beautiful easy half canter he had, but as you never knew when he would dive on to his nose, as if his legs had been cut off at the shoulder, you could never feel comfortable on him.

About the day after we got in to Brandfort we heard that a train-load of remounts had come up for our column, and I, amongst others, was told off to go down and detrain them. We had a grand morning's work, as they were a shy, frightened lot, rather handsome horses with beautiful silky coats; they said they were Hungarian horses. We got them all out and had batches of them told off to the different regiments. I was senior of our company, and I picked a very good-looking, showy mare; she would have made a beautiful carriage horse if you could have paired her.

I started off for camp on her at the head of my string, not "fancying" myself at all. The mare was curvetting about and showing herself, being glad to be out of the train. We were bare-backed, so I was glad she was a nice, good-natured animal. I filed past the flank of the camp like a fool, with her arching her neck and champing the bit. Of course the first thing that happened was that old Lloyd, our commanding officer, came out and looked her over and promptly commandeered her, and I got a heavy-footed, lumbering old beast with a head like a coalscuttle, and a canter that would fracture your skull!

Behold us, then, next day starting on our travels again, nearly every man remounted, from Major Lloyd (on my mare) down through Captain Leigh—who didn't ride as light as he used to, and had drawn two very serviceable weight-carrying cobs with good looks, which are difficult to get out here in conjunction with strength—to the little cockney recruit Van-der-steyn (bad name to be captured with), who had a great raking black mare that bounced him about like a pea on a drum! Van didn't care about "bahncing abaht like a blinding pancake," so swapped with a youngster named Digweed (we had a good collection of names in our company); but the mare ran away with "Chickweed," as they called him, twice in the morning, so the captain made me swap with him. This pleased me all right, as I was pretty tired of my old knacker. This brings me to my fourth remount, and she lasted till peace was declared, though I did not keep her all the time; but that is another story.

THE BLACK MARE

CHAPTER 15

"Incidents"

We went south-west from Brandfort this time, over new country, towards Kimberley. One day we came to a huge salt pan about two miles across, which looked like a huge dam as the white salt crust glistened like water. There were big salt workings here and a tremendous lot of sacks of salt piled, which we burnt—rather childish, I thought, as if any Boers wanted salt they only had to go down to the pan, where there was an inch of it crusted.

A report got about that the manager of the salt workings had buried a lot of money at his house, and men were digging and probing all over the place, like the treasure-seekers at home after the money buried by *Pearson's Weekly* and other enterprising papers! I don't think anyone found anything, though. We were having a lot of fun every day with the remounts. There were always some of them bolting or doing something. One used to insist, whenever he was watering at a dam, on wading out into the middle and lying down, the only way to stop him being to

jab him with a bayonet! He must have been a bathing-machine horse, I think—took to the water like a duck.

About a day's march north of Boshof we sighted a lot of wagons, and the guns dropped a couple of shells "across their bows" as a hint for them to pull up; but they went on, so the Mounted Infantry were put after them. When we got close we were fired on, so of course we let rip, and a few Boers cleared and left the wagons, which we found to be full of women, one of whom was shot dead. Well, was that our fault or the Joes, who must have known that they would be fired on if they did not stop, and especially if they fired on us?

Probably most of the "atrocities," worked up by Emily Hobhouse (who ought to be made to prove all her statements) and her sort, had the same sort of explanation. Anyway, her yarns about the concentration camps were utter rot; they lived in them in a way that used to make the "brutal soldiery's" mouths water when they came into a town after trekking. Our food (on the mounted) was generally good enough, but we never had shelter, often being wet through every and all nights for a week on end, and we never got enough sleep.

These persecuted people, however, were living in roomy, cool marquees, and were paid for doing things for themselves. Thus, if they wanted an oven to bake their bread in, the men made one, and got paid for it (this I know for a fact in some camps). As to the mortality among the children it must have been difficult in some places to get absolutely good water for such a crowd; but even then the doctors say the women would not use their prescriptions.

There was one case of a youngster with measles or chicken-pox, or something that the doctor prescribed for. On his next visit he found all his appliances on one side and the kid smothered all over with wet cow-dung!—one of the mothers' private recipes. It was foolish letting paper men interview women like Mrs. De Wet[1] and the wives of commandants—mostly very ig-

---

1. There was a great interview, in one paper, with Mrs. De Wet or Mrs. Botha, I'm not sure which.

142

norant, pig-headed people.

Of course, the pose of "persecuted martyrs" suited them down to the ground. After being bucolic country women all their lives they wouldn't miss the chance of posing as anything, and that was the only line to take. Can't you imagine "Mrs. Giles" under the same circumstances bewailing her position before the war, and saying that "Mr. Giles would be no husband of hers if he didn't fight to the death," and all the rot that Mrs. De Wet and Co. used to talk?

It's a curious thing that they don't hold to their word, now that Mr. De Wet, Botha, etc., are importing thoroughbred Hereford bulls and prize merino rams, and so on! (see *Johannesburg Star*). Besides, I've done a good deal of bringing in convoys to their camps, and the women were generally jolly enough, and would talk to the Tommies and seem satisfied with their rations, and in fact never seem to think they had a grievance till someone of the Hobhouse persuasion got hold of them.

Of course, a lot of them were sulky, but that was because they had the national hatred of the British and didn't like to see them winning—not on account of their personal treatment. Talking of women, it used to be a great thing to get on "women's *laager* guard"; it counted an outpost. All the wagons of the women (sometimes we had twenty or thirty) were *laager*ed up together, and the guard was on to keep it private more than to prevent escapes. I used to post my sentries, and then take a walk through the *laager* and have a look at all the different families, each round their own fire.

Drawing rations was the best fun. A corporal would come down from the supply camp with a wagon and shout "turn up for your rations," and you'd see all the fat old *frous* doubling up with their ration bags and crowd round, when he'd call their names—"Mrs. Du Toit," and Mother Du Toit would roll up and draw her lot, "Mrs. Van der Pomp," and so on.

Perhaps Mrs. "Van der Pomp's "would not be satisfactory; she wanted less bone and a little more suet or something, and there would be a great chattering and arguing, those who could talk

143

Mrs Prinsloo wants beef, and only a leg of muton left! (Ructions)

English all trying to translate for her, and explaining that Mrs. Pumperknickel (who couldn't understand what they were saying) had a sick daughter, so she could have the shin for beef tea and Mrs. Van der Pomp have the fat.

At last the worried corporal would fling lumps of fat and shin bones, etc., right and left, and let them fight it out. After supper they used to sing sometimes psalms but quite as often English songs—for our benefit, I suppose—a favourite one being "Oh, where is my wandering boy tonight?" Of which they knew the words but not the sense, in most cases, for they used to slur words and make two words into one, in a parrot-like way.

This was more the younger girls—the old ladies used to sit under the wagon tilt and drink coffee. A thing I could never understand was that on posting a sentry at 4 a.m., I would be shivering in a great coat, and it would be dark, yet these women used to be up, standing round a little fire drinking the everlasting coffee—this, when perhaps we did not trek that day.

Well, *revenons à nos moutons!* The night the woman unfortunately got shot, we camped under a rocky bluff which stood out like an island on the *veldt*, and I was on outpost. There was a strong outpost on the *kopje*, half my company being on, and I was on advanced post down a spur the other side. They were expecting the Boers up that side in the same way as they got the Yeomanry on Christmas day at Tweefontein, and we were cautioned to keep a sharp look out.

We kept seeing lights out in the *veldt* all night, but no one disturbed us. However, we had a bit of excitement, as just at daylight, from the top of the kop, we spotted some men coming for camp as hard as they could lick. These we made out to be a party of the night scouts: two Tommies and five Kaffirs, who had been out as usual all night getting information. We soon made out that they were being chased, and watched them with great excitement.

Gradually four drew ahead, and we could see the Boers, fifteen or twenty of them, were gaining on the other three. Presently they got up to them and surrounded them, and then we heard, pop—pop—pop—, three shots, and the Boers went off over the skyline again. In a few minutes the four rode in, two whites and two Kaffirs, and when we trekked that morning we came on the bodies of the other three Kaffirs laid out in a row by the side of the road with a bullet apiece in the brain. Joe always put out a Kaffir if he caught him, and was not particular about a white man of the night scouts, as they seemed to think night work was not fair.

After a couple of days' trek we came out on to a plain that looked familiar, and presently struck a river, which we followed up to a drift; this we suddenly realised was Koodoesrand Drift, where French had been when we had Cronje at Paardeberg, and on rounding the spur of the *kopje* that runs down to the river we could see Paardeberg ahead. The column camped at Koodoesrand and sent detachments off to all the *drifts* along the river—one regiment to Poplar Grove, one to the *kopjes* overlooking a small *drift* just above the *laager*, and my company to Paardeberg Drift.

We marched past the *laager*, and I rode over to have a look at it. It was very much as we had left it, except that the Kimberley people had decorated up the graves a bit. But the shell-proof trenches were there still, and an old wagon which was so riddled with bullets and splintered with shell that I suppose it would not have held together if moved.

I was on the advance-guard, and just caught them up in time to be sent on with ten men to get up on the kop overlooking the drift in case there were a few snipers about. We cantered on and climbed up the *kopje*, which is a pretty stiff climb, being all big boulders and very steep.

By the time we reached the top the advance-guard had come up and were filing down to the drift to water their horses. The drift was at the side of the *kopje*, so that it was commanded by the other side of the *kopje* as well as ours, and they ought to have given us time to get over to the other end. Just as they got to the drift there was a brisk little spatter of rifle fire from the foot of the *kopje* on the other side to where we had come up.

146

I just had time to see two loose horses gallop away from the *drift* as we doubled along the top of the *kop*, barking our shins and falling over rocks; but when we got to the further edge there were twelve Boers just mounting and riding leisurely off. We had a lot of fun banging at them, but only made them hurry a bit, not doing much damage I'm afraid. They got behind a ridge about 800 yards off and had a few snaps at us, and then rode off at the walk towards Klip Drift.

Presently a man came out from behind the same ridge and galloped towards us; when he came within range we let off at him of course, and there were little spurts of sand all round him, but he rounded the *kopje* and joined the company!—one of our own men, but I've never discovered how he got out there. He must have been almost amongst the Boers.

We camped here for about ten days with a post on the *kopje* and another on the drift. The general idea was that a big mob of Boers were being driven on to the Modder from the other side, and we were holding all the drifts. From Paardeberg you could see a tremendous distance, and we had a signalling station in communication with Kimberley and all the other detachments along the river, and used to report anything we saw. One day there was a thin trail of dust about twenty-five miles the other side of the river towards Springfontein, and gradually with glasses we made out wagons and Cape carts trekking south, with clouds of mounted men round.

This was probably our friends that we were waiting for, but it might also be one of our own columns, and Captain Leigh wanted to make sure. As this crowd was heading, they would pass about six miles from Klip Drift, where the river made a bend towards them; so Captain Leigh sent a lieutenant with a section or so to cross the drift, and go on till they got in touch, and see if they were British or Boers. Rather a nasty job, as country looks very different from the top of a *kopje* to when you're crossing it, little hillocks becoming great rises that might hide an army corps. I was one of this picnic, though it was Sergeant Williams' section that went; I forget how I came to be sent.

ADVANCE-GUARD GOING FOR A *KOPJE*

We soon got to Klip Drift, about four miles off, and crossed. After that we had to look out, as if we got cut off from the *drift*, our only chance would be to try and break through to Jacobsdal thirty miles off, and it was bad country. I was on advanced screen again, and at every farm we came on traces of Joe, where he had roasted some *mealie* cobs or something.

At last we got to the big rise where we expected to see the commando from, and they sent up word to me to rush the little *kopje* on the top. Just as I was signalling to my commando to gallop, I saw a Boer on a white horse drive about six cattle out from a belt of scrub and take them behind the *kopje* at the canter. I thought things looked pretty hopeful; however, we were well under way now, so I thought I might as well let her rip.

There was no one on the *kopje*, but down in the valley the other side was a thick belt of scrub and a white wagon-tilt showing up amongst the trees. I sent back word about this, and then we began discussing the wagon. Now a wagon, with its possibilities of loot was to any mounted troop what a jam tin is to flies, and my men were very anxious to get down to it; but it was a rotten place, as not only could a regiment have been in the bush but there were *kopjes* all round quite close, and we could easily have been cut off.

However, I reflected that the officer would probably send me down, when he came up, to find out all about this wagon, and I decided not to wait, as it would only give them more time to get ready for us; so opening out we charged down on the timber. I went straight past the wagon and had a look through the scrub, then came back and proceeded to interview the old chap who was in charge. There was the old man, and his daughter of about eighteen, and two boys—no signs of the white horse and cattle, which I did not like.

The old man told me his donkeys were grazing under a *kopje* to the right, and I told him to send for them and sent one man with his boys, for I meant to take the wagon back with me. Of course we were keeping a sharp lookout, and presently a man said: "Who are those chaps, Corporal?" and pointed out about twenty coming through the scrub and making for the *kopje* under which the donkeys were! I knew they were not our patrol, and didn't care who else they were. I got my men mounted on the edge of the scrub, and then went to call the man back who was after the donkeys. It was not necessary, however, as they got a few short range snaps at him that fetched him back pretty quick.

The remainder cleared then for the *nek*, where we expected to find our patrol, and I and the other fellow came on after as hard as we could. The other chap was a bit behind me, and he swears that as he passed the wagon the old fellow got out his rifle from somewhere (we had not had time to search the wagon) and had a couple of snipes at him!

The Boers on the *kopje* were making things hum, and we were not wasting any time. I expected to be cut off, for we had to pass over a *nek* on the same *kopje*; so imagine my joy when a man just in front of me, after swaying about a lot on his horse's neck, fell off! I made sure, of course, that he was badly hit, and knew I should be blamed for going down to the wagon; but the man got up and ran. I let him run till we got over a ridge, as I did not want a repetition of the Corporal White affair. Then I pulled up and told him to get up behind me. The mare, however, who was always pretty full of herself, wouldn't stand, and the man was badly puffed.

The consequence was that, struggling to get up, he pulled me round saddle and all. I had not bargained for waiting so long, so

was uncommonly relieved when another man brought the loose horseback, having luckily caught it as it was galloping past him.

I expected to see the Joes' heads bobbing over the rise every minute, so did not dismount for my helmet which had dropped off in the struggle, but went on; in fact, the mare, which was an awful coward under fire, fairly got away with me, and I had to right the saddle by standing in the off stirrup till it came round.

The man was not hit at all, which annoyed me; he had simply fallen off—why, I don't know. We did not find the patrol till we got back to Klip Drift; they had apparently gone straight back when I reported the wagon. That was the last wagon I tried to capture on my own!

Next day a party of Boers came down and crossed the drift by the old *laager*, and about fifteen of us were sent to take up a position on the ridge from which the big guns fired into the *laager*. However, they struck the Yeomanry in the *kopjes*, and were driven over the river again. The big mob of Boers were hanging about now in the *kopjes* opposite Paardeberg Kop, and every day a corporal and ten men had to go off to Klip Drift four miles off, which was quite out of sight or communication with the company, and stop there till next morning, not so much to stop the Boer's crossing as to let ours know if they had crossed. (If the post came in, all right, but if their mangled remains were found they would know that Joe had crossed !)

It was rather pleasant in the daytime, being away on your own: there were farms close round, so we could send a man for eggs, fowls, etc., and we would be able to get away all right if Joseph did come. But at night it was different: pitch dark, and generally a noisy wind, perhaps rain, so that the Boer advance could ride over you before you saw or heard them. It was rather fun sitting up on a *kopje*, watching Boers riding about in twos and threes, wondering if they would come to the drift so that we could have a go at them.

One day from Paardeberg, the post on the top reported a single horseman to have crossed the river between us and Klip Drift, and to be going in the direction of Kimberley; so the men who had horses handy bustled off after him, and we watched developments from the berg. At first the man, whoever he was, tried to get away, but his horse was outpaced, and we soon saw two or three close round him, and presently they brought him in. He was a dispatch rider from Jacobsdal looking for our force, a Kaffir on a poor, miserable little pony not more than eighteen months old, I should think—knock-kneed, cow-hocked, and generally broken-down looking.

The Kaffir must have had a nerve to chance his life on her, with the country swarming with Boers who would shoot Kaffirs on suspicion, or without suspicion for that matter. However, the little pony had brought him thirty miles in a surprisingly short time, and when we had fed them both and directed the Kaffir to Pilcher's head-quarters, she ambled off again as if she had a lot left in her.

THE KAFFIR DESPATCH RIDER

Chapter 16

The Fight Near Bultfontein

We heard in a day or two that Knox or someone had got most of the convoy of the Boers and broken them up. Those that got through broke south past Koffyfontein, none coming our way; so we all collected together and went off again nearly the way we had come—north, past Boshof.

We had for one of our guides from Kimberley a commandant (Niel, I think) who had been with the Boers who chased us at Bothaville when Neilson was killed. He said there were six or eight hundred of them; they had been sending for them all the night before when we had the night attack, sending gallopers as far as Venterskroon, nearly to Potchefstroom. He had come in and surrendered—a "hands opper," as the Boers call them.

As we drew away from the river we came out into a plain surrounded by rough-looking *kopjes* with thick bush all round them, and as the left flank-guard passed along the range on the left we could hear them getting sniped at a good deal. We were not advance-guard, but you never know where you will be sent if any fighting comes on, so I was watching the advance-guard draw up to the *kopjes* in front with considerable misgivings. (I used to hate fighting in bush and broken land—with reason, too.)

As I expected, before they got fired on even, we were ordered up—I thought, to reinforce them; but no such luck. Two sections (Sergeants Murdoch and Williams) cantered straight through the advance-guard and went for the line of rocky bluffs "on our lonesome."

Why the advance-guard couldn't have done it, I don't know. Murdoch came over to me and told me to take roughly half the section (we were extended to about twenty paces) round the left of a bluff, and he would go round the right; so I hollo'd about eight to come my way, and we dived into the scrub round the base of the *kop*, just hearing a shot on Murdoch's side to cheer us up.

We were to meet Murdoch behind the bluff, so I thought if I had to go I'd better go quick, and was bustling round the bluff, falling into *donga*s and over rotting tree trunks in great style, when suddenly we rattled out on to a hollow full of ox-wagons being hurriedly inspanned and Cape carts driving off. We had struck a small *laager*. They had heard us coming, too, and we were greeted by Boers behind all the trees on the other side of the *laager*. There was a big *donga*, cut deep by rain water just on the left, so I turned short round and made for it (the men didn't want telling to do the same!).

At the first whiz of a bullet the mare as usual went ratty, and now, instead of getting into the *donga*, she went for it full steam and made a buck leap over, considerably unsettling me! However, I got her back into it, and we proceeded to snipe the wagons and wait for reinforcements. Presently they came in the shape of the remainder of the company, who came up on a little conical *kopje* behind us. By this time all the wagons and Boers were out of sight in the bush, bar one ox-wagon, and Captain Leigh was reviling me at the top of his shout for not going on and capturing it!

All very well, but he had not seen all I had; besides, I'd been capturing wagons before, quite recently, and you can see the result on previous pages! However, I was not going to argue the point, so collected my bold band of *desperadoes* (I only had three left, the remainder had faded away down the *donga* in search of better cover!) and made a dash into the bush as if it would take a commando to stop me. As soon, however, as I was out of sight of the conical *kopje*, I pulled up behind a thick bush and awaited developments.

Presently, the Norfolk company came up at the gallop, and I attached myself to them and went on after the rear wagon, which was just disappearing over a *nek*. I got up within about seventy yards of the wagon (we were scattered about all over the bush, of course), and finding no one fired at me I dismounted and had some snaps at it; but every time I fired the mare would bound backwards, dragging me with her, so I don't expect I did much damage. After three or four attempts I smote her heavily on the nose with the butt, to quieten her, but as that had no effect I went on up to the rise.

The first thing I saw the other side was the wagon deserted, so I being the only one near it (the rest were away to the left a bit), and as there were apparently no Boers about, and no bush this side either, I started to lead the mare down to the wagon, thinking there might be some loot. But the Joes were covering it from a *kopje* in front, as I might have expected, and I had to lie on my face behind a rock till I was relieved!

The column was coming up by this time, and not being in a hurry to join the company (it was always better fun in a skirmish to be on your own), I went off with a few bold spirits in pursuit of the Boers, not in the least expecting to find them. Coming

MUSKETRY UNDER DIFFICULTIES

155

suddenly over a rise overlooking a farm with a big dam, to our surprise we got a grand view of the commando cantering off towards Boshof. We did not pursue them any farther, but sat on the rocks and sniped into the brown of them at about 700 yards, till a man on a corner of the rise reported three or four wagons stealing away to the left with no mounted men about.

This was "just our mark," and off we went again, each man in command of himself, and opened fire on the wagons at about 600, when out tumbled women of all ages and sizes and took cover behind ant-hills, rocks, etc., as if they had been born to it. Of course we stopped firing then, and went up and got the wagons. Coming back, I fell in with the company, so had to re-join. Old "Shylock," Sergeant Henson's horse, which had been trekking since some time before Bothaville, was hit through the neck, but it never seemed to do him much harm.

We camped at the farm with the dam, but there was soon one of those hated rumours going about about a night march, and it turned out that two companies—ourselves and, I think, the Lincolns—were for it! We were shoved along pretty fast nearly all night till we must have been fifteen or twenty miles from the column, when just before dawn we pulled up at a big farm, with great cattle *kraals*, stuck out on a rolling plain, where you could see for ten miles round. We got our horses in the *kraals* and outhouses out of sight and kept dark ourselves, as Captain Leigh explained to us that we had come through the Boers in the night and the column was going to drive them on to us.

We did not see anything till about 11 a.m., when there was a big dust-cloud on the horizon, out of which emerged a herd of cattle. We sent two men out, and the two or three youngsters who were driving the oxen thought they were Boers, so were easily captured, and the herd yarded just in time to go for another small herd; and so we kept on all day now—a herd of cattle and now sheep, with an occasional chase after a Cape cart, till we had about twenty prisoners, and all the *kraals* full of cattle—a fairly successful move. The Boers got wind of us and passed well on either side out of range, but we had a good deal to show when the column came up that evening.

About this time I nearly earned the heart- felt thanks of the column for shooting the Provost-Marshal (the most unpopular man in the column, as he is always trying to stop looting and breaking up houses for wood, etc.!). It happened in this way: I was advance-guard, and when we came to the camp was on a *kopje* in front till they got the outpost out, so that of course I was supposed to be the most advanced party of the column; when, therefore, I saw five or six horsemen come away from a farm about two miles in front of us, and come toward us (they could not see us or the camp), we let them have about half a magazine full each, and they galloped for a *kopje* on our right, subsequently coming round to "rear up" on me.

I guessed what was wrong as soon as I heard the "Who's in charge here?" in the rasping voice which some officers think necessary to use when they want to overawe a subordinate. It was the provost-marshal and an undersized little creature who used to follow him round and call himself assistant provost-mar-shal!

After he had made some remarks, more or less appropriate, I told him I considered I was not to blame for believing the advance screen to be in front, and they retired with a parting shot from the little man, "Dem'd bad shooting, anyway." I felt inclined to ask him why he had galloped for cover so fast in that case, but refrained. The provost-marshal was sore on the subject because the 5th Mounted Infantry (Royal Irish, I think) had sworn in his hearing, after a similar occurrence, that they would shoot him next time, whether they knew him or not, if he got in front of their advance.

We halted for a day or two near Boshof while some of the column went in for supplies. We were on the edge of a big dry pan, and one night I was on outpost on the other side of the pan; there had been a lot of sniping into camp at night, so we were looking out. I left the horses under the bank and lay out on top, all of us up by the sentry; in fact, I had the sentry lying down, too, as this was just the place for a Boer to come and snipe into camp, the lights of which you could see spread out on the slope half a mile away at the other side of the pan.

We were all lying in a row with the sentry at the end, and I went to sleep after posting the man at 12 p.m., leaving him and the relieved sentry talking in undertones, they being the two on my right. Shortly afterwards I was awakened by a terrific double report in my ear. Of course, we had our rifles alongside us, so I was ready without even throwing off the blanket. The two men said they had heard a horseman coming and had waited till he was just on us and they could see him looming up in the dark, and when they fired he had turned and galloped for it. I could not hear anything myself, but that may have been owing to having two rifles let off in my ear!

We arrived without much excitement a day's march south of the little town of Bultfontein. There was supposed to be a Boer force of considerable strength here, and the 5th Mounted Infantry went on, on a night march, in the same way that we had when we captured the cattle, to make a night attack. The town was empty, though, and they took up positions in the old trenches (the town had been occupied, but was abandoned) to capture any Boers we might drive in.

The only result, however, was two boys of about fourteen, one the son of Commandant Britz, I think, and the other a "by woner "or yokel. They were "despatch riders," if you please! Mounted on rough little Boer tats, the swagger one of the two

A CAPTURE

had a carbine, and the other an old muzzle-loading horse-pistol. I was on guard down town that night, and they were handed over to me by the big R.I. sentry. The commandant's son could talk English, and was very communicative.

We made a fortified sort of camp at Bultfontein, and half the column stayed there, while the remainder of us, about a regiment and half of Mounted Infantry, and half the Yeomanry, with about three guns and transport to correspond, set off north towards our old happy hunting grounds round Bothaville. There had been a smash up somewhere on the Vaal, some camp or column having been cut up a bit, and we thought we were going to trek up to the Vaal to take part in a punitive move. We had a mid-day halt the first day out, in a little hollow with a farm and a dam in it, called Orange Pan.

There had been a tremendous lot of *veldt* fires about during the morning's trek. Just before we came to camp we had passed a small iron building, so that when after we had got off-saddled, etc., we heard a lot of hammering, tapping sort of noises behind the ridge, we thought it was some of the fellows breaking up the iron building for wood. Every now and then someone would say, "I believe that's firing," but the remainder kept saying, "No, only the iron house," so that it had been going on for some time when Pilcher came flying over from the farm where an orderly had found him, I suppose shouting, "Get out on the ridge at once, we're heavily engaged!"

Then there was a scramble. Some started to run up to the ridge, others going for their horses, and galloping up bare-backed (I got my horse, never being fond of running), gunners hooking in two horses and flogging up to the rise, no orders being given except to "get out there," so that very soon the ridge was lined and a very sharp little engagement taking place.

There was a Kaffir hut on the rise, and seeing the first gun going for that I went with them, and as soon as we got to the top could see the whole situation at a glance. The Yeomanry had been rear-guard, and they had done very well, sending in their horses and retiring on foot themselves. One of them passed

GETTING OUT ON THE RIDGE

A SKETCH OF THE ENGAGEMENT FROM THE KAFFIR HUT

through by me shot through the nose!

The *veldt* fires were the cause of the trouble, Britz, if it were he, having taken a leaf out of Kemp's book and attacked the rear under cover of the smoke. In the sketch earlier the black patch represents burnt ground, with Boers dodging in and out of the smoke. We had scarcely got up when the major in charge of the gun was shot through the groin, and we put him behind the Kaffir hut, from where he kept giving orders, which the young lieutenant left in charge took no notice of, evidently thinking the old man was out of action. Then a gunner was shot dead, and someone threw a helmet over his face.

Altogether it was pretty warm; there was a continual whiz of bullets coming over the rise; but there were a lot of us, and the Boers were getting it warm, too, loose horses careering all over the place. This was the second place I saw case shot used, Bothaville being the other. At first the youngster at the gun was going on shrapnel. I could hear him, "With shrapnel, load—at 150" etc., then at one hundred, and the shrapnel seemed to burst almost simultaneously with the report of the gun. At last he said, "D—n it, give 'em case!" and then you could see it plough up great furrows of dust on the black background of burnt grass.

By the time the other two guns got well into action, the Boers had had enough, and drew off, leaving some of their dead and a lot of loose horses. Some of us wanted to go out and get the horses, and incidentally to go through the saddle-bags; but they would not let us, and a civilian guide coming up went out and caught the pick of the ponies for himself, and got great stores of tobacco, biltong, clothing, etc., out of the saddle-bags, much to Tommy's disgust. He brought in word that a man who looked like a commandant, was still alive, though badly burnt by the *veldt* fire; so they sent an ambulance round and brought in all the dead and wounded.

The only one alive was this commandant, and he was badly mauled with shrapnel in the head and burnt afterwards; he died that night without recovering consciousness. We only had two or three killed and a few wounded, and next morning, after burying the dead, we trekked back the way we had come.

At nearly every farm we found Boer dead and wounded, collecting altogether sixteen dead, I don't know how many wounded, and a woman told us how it came about. The day before a big commando had passed her farm, travelling hard (her farm was a bit off our previous track) after us, and the commandant, who pulled up to speak to her, said, "There's a khaki patrol just gone over there; we'll fetch it back presently," and told her to have some food ready for him in a few hours or so! Evidently they had seen our dust leaving Bultfontein, and noticing the camp still there thought we were only a small patrol! which accounted for the determined way they had come on.

We left Bultfontein on our left and struck out west after these people. The first day after a short chase we got a few wagons full of women. These we left under a *kopje*, taking their trek chassis with us so that they could not move; and as we left them three days' full rations, coffee, sugar, etc., I expect they used to have a sort of standing "At home" for all the Boers in the district. Next day we came on their rear-guard holding a *kopje* covered with bush like Krantz Kop, but some of the 5th rushed them and they cleared out. (I got a turkey from a farm at the foot of the *kopje*.) Then we got into thick bush, and I was advance-guard when we got to a farm, nearly on the borders of the Free State, I should think.

There was a donkey wagon outspanned there, and we got one Boer and his family. He said they were in a bad way, a lot of them wounded and short of supplies. There was a tremendous lot of wool in this farm, and in a shed full of it I found twenty-three eggs, which Guyatt and I ate that night. I'm not sure that we did not eat half the turkey as well!

We went back then to where we had left the wagons, which were there still, and on back to the remainder of the column at Bultfontein. Guyatt, foraging round for wood to cook with, fell foul of the provost-marshal, who was flying around making prisoners right and left. But for some very smart flank movement he would have had Guyatt; he dashed into the door as

An encounter with the provost marshall

Guyatt dived out of the window with a load of match-boarding or something.

We went into Brandfort again then. Rather an amusing event occurred on the way. One of the duties of the *Laager* Guard was to turn the boys out at 3 a.m. to graze the wagon bullocks, and once when I was on, one of the boys cleared off with his span to the Boers. (Of course, we were not responsible after we had turned them out and called the conductor.) The women on the wagon laughed and jeered, and boasted that they had told the boy to go; they stopped laughing, though, when Pilcher sent a weak team of mules over from the supply, and made them fling most of their furniture, etc., off to lighten the wagon! No more teams were lost.

After a day or two at Brandfort we struck out east of the line, and made for our old happy hunting grounds round the Kovannaberg, and camped under a *kopje* near Allandale. The night we arrived here one of the Norfolks' officers strolled up on the *kopje* just above camp, and got shot through the hand by an enterprising sniper.

There were a lot of table-lands all round here, and one day there was a great *indaba*, all the officers and senior non-coms, being called up to Pilcher's tent; and that night we all went off on our own, one section to each table-land in sight, pretty well! My section going to the one on the extreme right. I got left, as the man with the pack-horse got into difficulties, his load of ammunition, rations, etc., coming loose or something; and as the *kopje* we were going to was about five miles off, daylight found us two still a mile or two off it, having called at every other available one during the night inquiring for "No. 4 section Hants Company." We did not lose time, and any Boers could have gathered us in that saw us.

I found Sergeant Murdoch ensconced on the top of the *krantz*, and we had a very good time up there; we had a splendid view and nothing to do but watch. We were up there three days, while Pilcher took the remainder of the column into the circle formed by us, and routed round after the Boers. The nights were the only jumpy times, for if a mob of Boers had happened to want to come up on our *krantz* in the dark, we could not stop them, as it was too big to hold, and we were never sure if moving might not show us to be doing outpost for a couple of hundred Boers!

I had Conan Doyle's book, *The Great Boer War*, and it was rather funny sitting up there in the rocks reading about the war in the same way that one reads about the Crimea, whilst I could hear Pilcher firing away like blazes in the *krantzes*, and if I had ridden a mile from the *kopje* would have been engaged in a Boer war of my own.

There were little caves up on our *krantz* formed by two or three great rocks leaning against each other, and we lived in these. Beautifully warm they were, when a cold wind was sweeping over the *kopje*.

Pilcher came up to us one day; he had a guide with him, an old Scotchman who had been a travelling pedlar all round this district before the war, so knew it by heart and all the people in it. They had often sent in messages to him after the manner of the Matabele, etc., telling him what they would do to him if they caught him. (I mention him because they got him that night, poor devil!) He often used to go out with the night scouts, and this night he went out from the column camp. We heard a lot of firing at a farm way on our left, and heard afterwards that they had stumbled on a hornet's nest.

While the scouts were in this farm gathering information,

READING ABOUT *THE GREAT BOER WAR*

the Boers came down off the *kopje*, and they had to scatter. Old Carmichael (I think his name was) got cut off from camp. He gave them about five miles' chase; but they caught him, and we found his body, with bullets all over him, a day or two after.

There was a man of the Buffs (5th Mounted Infantry) captured the same night, and they gave him a bad quarter of an hour, too. They took him to Allandale to the commandant (I don't know whether it was De Wet or not). The commandant seemed to be in a bad temper, and said, "Do you belong to these '*verdomde*' night-riding people?" The Buff thought it was no use denying, as he was caught at about 12 p.m., so he said he was.

"Fetch my rifle," said the other. The cockney admits that he felt pretty uncomfortable.

When the rifle was brought the Boer cocked it and said, "Now if I let you off, will you promise not to fight again? "Of course, Tommy knew that the commandant knew that he would have to, so he said: "If I get back to the column I shall have to fight again, whether I want to or not."

"I knew that," said the other; "if you had told a lie, I'd have shot you." He then handed his rifle to another Boer and said, "Bring my *sjambok*!"

This did not worry the Buff at all, as he said afterwards, "They could bring all the —— *sjamboks* in the camp so long as they took away that —— gun!"

However, the commandant began telling him about some men he had captured once, whom he had made swear all sorts of impossible things, and got so friendly that by the time the *sjambok* arrived he would not use it, but let the man go. The way they did so was curious, though. They took him about five miles off and handed him over to another post, who handed him on, and so on all day till they finally let him go about eight miles from camp.

If their object was to make him lose his bearings they were wasting their time, as both the 7th and 5th Mounted Infantry knew the Eastern Free State as well as the Boers did. Some of his escorts were boys that he could have mastered with one hand;

but they had rifles, of course, and he had not, and the younger Joes were always ready to pull off on any provocation; in fact, lots of released prisoners say they owe their release to the old chaps, for the youngsters of fourteen and fifteen wanted to shoot them!

Guyatt had an adventure from the *kopje*. Sergeant Murdoch sent him with some message to another section on a *krantz* away in the distance. Guyatt always had a good horse, as he would always take a rough one, nothing pleasing him better than a few minutes' bucking every morning. He went off all right, but once down in the broken ground he lost sight of the *krantz* he was making for, and had to make for it the best way he could. After a time he came to one that looked like the right one, and shouted up, "Is that No. — section?"

"Yes," came the answer.

"Is Mr. So-and-so up there?"

"Yes," again.

So he was dismounting to go up when the voice shouted, "Come up here!"

This struck him as strange when he was just going up, and something in the pronunciation was queer, too, so he hesitated,

Under Escort

when there was such an eager chorus of "Come on," "Come up here," etc., that he mounted again and was edging off, laughing (he always was laughing, and a thing like that would just tickle him).

They saw the game was up, so there was a shout of laughter all over the *kopje*, and a brisk fusillade. Guyatt "Got!" Altogether a most jovial encounter!

When we got word to go in, the camp was about ten miles off; we could just see the lights in the distance, so we decided to make a night march of it, as we did not want the Boers to spot us. We had a pretty happy march, too, as we went across country, and kept coming to bottomless *donga*s and swamps, etc.; however, we got in all right.

CHAPTER 17

I Get Enteric

We all went on an excursion into the mountains behind the Korannaberg next. One broiling hot day we had just got on a ridge, when some Boers opened fire from a Kaffir *kraal* on us. One of our chaps (Private Mansell) took cover behind an ant-heap, but a bullet hit that and bust it up, hitting him in the mouth; he was much astonished, as ant-heaps were considered pretty good cover. Going on a message I struck a farm with a splendid orange grove, and had a glorious feed. Later that day we got home on them with howitzers. There was a gang of them on the corner of a *krantz* giving the advance-guard beans, when they sent a couple of shells over from the column, and, pitching just right (lyddite they were), killed eleven Boers. We could see these shells going over, and it was exciting to watch them.

After knocking round for a bit, we found ourselves at Thaba'nchu, and we camped a few miles out on the De Wet's

THABA'NCHU,

dorp road. Here we ended our connection with Pilcher, as we marched off (only our company) next morning to Bloemfontein.

We couldn't make out what was happening. We camped up at the Mounted Infantry rest camp in Bloemfontein for one night, and were very busy drawing horses, rations, etc., and new mules for our wagon, which dispelled the wild idea that we were being disbanded. Three of our beauties, when they found they were to trek again, stowed away in a truck for Capetown, with a box of biscuits and some bully beef. They did not know that every truck was searched systematically by the railway police, so were hauled out; and as we had marched, they were court-martialled for desertion, and got six months—two of them escaped from the Bloemfontein Prison afterwards, but were caught again and sent down to the breakwater at Capetown.

We marched down the line towards Springfontein, this being a sort of drive, and we forming the right-hand unit. Pilcher was stretched away across to the Caledon river. Nothing happened to us, naturally, as we were alongside the line all the way.

When we got to Edenberg we set out due west, some of the rest of the 7th coming with us to see us safe past Nieuhondt and Hertzog's hunting ground round Jagersfontein. We knew by this

THE STOWAWAYS DISCOVERED

time that we were going to join Plumer's column, as he had applied for some regulars, his column consisting solely of Australians and New Zealanders. We did great execution on this march amongst the stock. We used to round up hundreds of sheep and drive them into a stone *kraal*, then turn the men in with bayonets, axes, or anything and massacre the lot—a horrible business, and I'm not sure that it was necessary; perhaps it was, though.

We were pretty jumpy at this time, for we were only a small party, and a big mob of Boers were trekking down from the north, and we were not sure we would not just strike them. However, we arrived at Poplar Grove without adventure, where Plumer's column was lying, and the old 7th went back to Pilcher, leaving us and some Yeomanry with Plumer. We moved across and joined him that night.

Some of the 5th Q.I.B. (Queensland Imperial Bushmen) came over to our lines. I think they thought we were just out—though we couldn't have looked like it—as they were inclined to swagger, and I think had an idea that they could do a bit of horse-lifting from us; but they soon found they were wrong, and we always got on very well with both Queenslanders and New Zealanders, though they were not so good as the first contingents: none of the irregulars were—the first yeomanry lots were all right, whilst the less said about some of the last the better.

We went into Modder River station, leaving Paardeberg on our left. We passed the scene of the Magersfontein disaster, too, and I had a good look at it. It is easy to see how the thing happened when you see the place. The *kopje* comes in a half-moon from the line (to Kimberley) nearly down to the river, the road to Paardeberg passing round the foot of the *kopje* between it and the river.

About one hundred yards out from the foot of the *kopje* was a trench stretching the whole length from the line to the end of the *kopje* without a break, save where the road crossed. All the earth from the trench had been levelled off, so that you could not see it even in the daytime till you were on top of it. In front of that again, about fifteen yards, was a wire fence.

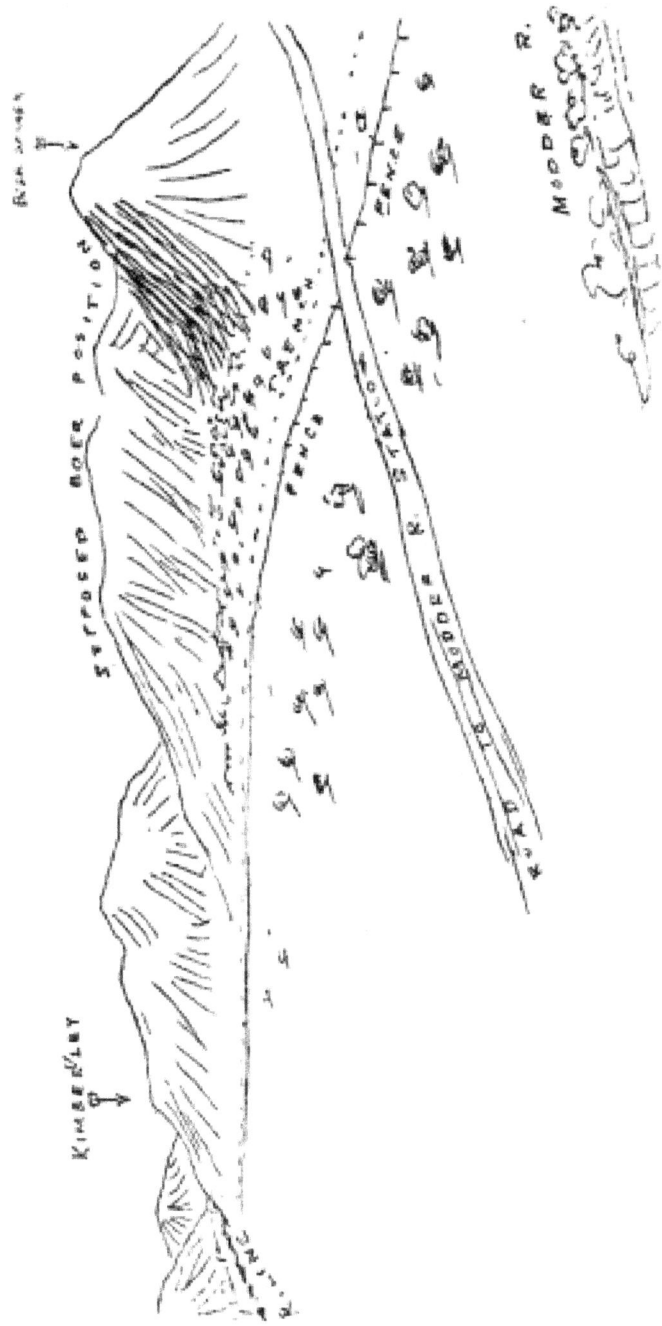

Magersfontein

The sketch shown of course is fore-shortened a lot, but it gives you an idea. The troops advanced in close formation along the road or parallel to it, thinking the Boers were on the *kopje*, which no doubt they could just see looming up in the dark. The front companies (they were in quarter column of companies) struck the fence; they dare not shout orders, so the rear companies kept closing up till it must have been hard enough work to keep from being spiked on the barbed wire, and then the Joes not twenty paces off opened fire! The graves were all just in front of the fence. I met a Boer afterwards in Koffyfontein, named Ferreira, who was there. He says they held their fire till they could make out the helmets—you would not do that on a dark night over twenty paces.

We kept hanging round Modder River for some time, going for short treks out towards Boshof , over the same ground that we covered after leaving Paardeberg with Pilcher the last time. On one occasion a Q.I.B. shot himself dead accidentally. He was coming down from an outpost on the identical *kopje* from which Captain Leigh had exhorted me to go on and capture the wagon.

On the same trek, a corporal and three men (Q.I.B.) were lost by the same trick that Guyatt had been too "slim" for in the Korannaberg. The Boers called them up on to a *kopje* in English, and shot them at point-blank range. Then from the same *kopje* that I had sniped the provost-marshal from, two of the Yeomanry on advance-guard were wounded.

The last time we went in to Modder station we were taking women in and burning the houses, and at a farm in the bush we struck a woman by herself. We told her to get ready her kit as we were going to take her in to a concentration camp, and she made ready all right. After her wagon moved off, our fellows fired the house. When she saw the smoke, she asked what it was. "Oh, that's your house going up," said one of the guard, and with a yell the woman made a buck-leap off the wagon, sprinted back to the farm, and lugged her old man out from under the floor!!

Our next move was out to Jacobsdal, which I had not seen since the general advance. We camped just by the town on the Riet River, and I had a bath in a rash moment! That night I electrified my sub-section by refusing to eat, a thing I had not done since the first day or two on the boat! Next morning I could not get warm, so wore my great coat along on the road, though the sun would peel the skin off your neck. Weston remonstrated with me, said all the column were laughing at me.

This annoyed me, and I d——d the column, and I'm not sure that I didn't d—n him too; anyway, he remarked that if I was mad I'd better go sick at once, so I took him at his word and rode over to the ambulance and reported sick to the doctor. He was an old Indian; evidently had a liver, for he would not let me on the ambulance—said he'd see me at the half-way halt. So I rode along with the ambulance till we halted at a dam, when I off-saddled and lay down under a wall feeling pretty sick.

No one took any notice of me till they started to move off. I was pretty comfortable where I was and did not make a move, much to the distress of the old black mare, who got very fidgety when she saw the remainder all moving off. Presently, the doctor spotted me and came and took my temperature, which was 104; then he could not do enough—got me into the ambulance, told off a man to look after my horse, gave me milk, and all sorts of things.

That night we got to Koffyfontein, and next morning they trundled me off into the town and dumped me at a nice little cottage hospital—beds with sheets, and all the luxuries you can imagine. The K.O.S.B. militia were stationed here, and one of their old soldiers was hospital orderly, and a civilian doctor named Hunter. Captain Leigh and Sergeant-Major Weston both came to look me up next day as the column went through.

I had been reported as a bad case of enteric, and they were both very anxious to cheer me up, which was quite unnecessary, as I didn't believe myself that I was so bad as they made out, and the prospect of a few weeks in bed with plenty of food, and no rainy nights on outposts (I soon discovered my mistake about plenty of food) would have cheered me up under any circumstances; so after exhorting Weston to buck up and allow no slackness in the company, I turned over for another nap, feeling that I had done uncommonly well for myself. Poor old Weston! Next time I saw him I was visiting him in hospital.

There was another "enteric" in the ward, and we were the only two at first. The old Militia drunk used to have great sport with us. It was a great joke of his to tell us in a confidential and beery whisper, that the doctor only gave us so many days to live; then the old scoundrel would go off chuckling to himself. He took a fancy to me, though, and at last was good enough to prophecy that I would pull through, but the other chap would die, in both of which "tips" he was right, though how far his dismal forebodings helped the other chap I don't know. I was supposed to be on milk from the first, but as soon as the doctor was away, the old beggar would fetch me in rousing nips, not forgetting himself. "Mon," he'd say, "tak a pull at this; fill dae ye all the gude i' th' world."

He got the sack finally for being unable to explain the decrease in the hospital spirits, and I missed him badly. Two hospital nurses and an R.A.M.C. orderly came from Kimberley then, as we got some more cases in from some column that was trekking round there. Most of them were Yeomanry, M.M.R. (Metropolitan Mounted—more commonly "mahntid"—Rifles) and the peaceful serenity which had prevailed during the old fellow's reign was broken up. These nurses were always wanting to scrub out the wards or change the sheets or something, which Donal' or whatever his name was, had considered quite unnecessary. He used to stroll in with a soft broom, and after a couple of sweeps he'd spit, and start expatiating on the time he was in the "Cawmeron Hielanders" (I think his corps had been). "Before ye wor chist measurement, laddie," he'd add.

They were a sporting lot, these Border militia. One of them, "Big Jock Murray," came into hospital with a broken ankle. He had been indulging in the hotel, and walking home to his outpost, which was the other side of the big diamond mine; he had

In hospital

walked over the edge, dropping about seventy feet on to loose gravel!

Several wounded came in from, I think, a Colonel White or Williams's column three officers, two shot through the body, and one (Buist, I think his name was, of the H.L.I.) through the eye, which he had to have removed. He was about 6 ft. 7 in. in height.

I used to be tremendously thirsty, and they would only give me about a wineglassful of champagne and brandy (this was when I was at the worst). I could often hear a tap running, so one night I thought it out that if I could only find that tap I'd have a glorious drink. I cruised about for a long time (this was in the old militiaman's time—he did not do night-nursing), but I could not find it, luckily; if I had I would have killed myself. When I got well, I discovered it just outside the door!

When I was convalescent I had a good time; used to go where I liked inside the outpost lines, watching the ladies playing tennis with mine managers, etc. And there was often a cricket match, and a concert in the Town Hall. You would never think the town was besieged (it took a column to bring supplies out to us), but for little incidents that happened periodically. One day there was a fight outside with Hertzog, and as they fetched our wounded in, a Dutch woman—Koffyfontein is very Dutch, of course—was standing at her door clapping her hands like a fool, so that no one could feel sorry for her when one of the end wagons turned out to contain her husband, dead! Quite poetical justice he was one of Hertzog's *burghers*.

Nieuhondt lived in Koffyfontein; his family was there at this time. Hertzog used to send in messages often that he was coming back that way at such and such a time, and would then take the herd of cattle (they had to go out under a grazing guard); and one time he kept his word, and cleared with the lot! But a column took them back the same day.

There was a Colonial doing intelligence officer. He used to go out with six or eight Kaffirs and scout about. One day he didn't come back, so next day they sent the ambulance out and found his six boys shot and laid out by the side of the road, no sign of him! He turned up a fortnight after. After his boys had been caught he led the Boers a good chase, but they shot his horse and got him. They asked him who he was (luckily there were no Koffyfontein men there).

Of course, if they had known he was an "Africander," they would have shot him at once; so he said he was a K.O.S.B. militiaman, and nearly broke his jaw trying to talk Scotch! It must have been very funny, though I don't suppose he saw the joke. Anyway, they were taking him to Nieuhondt's camp, and Nieuhondt knew him all his life pretty well, so he thought it was all up; but they fell in with an S.A.C. patrol, and left him; and he went into Edenburg with the patrol, coming home by rail via De Aar and Modder River.

I would have liked to stay in Koffyfontein and get his billet, but it seemed all of us convalescents had to go into Kimberley to be either passed "fit "or invalided home. Meanwhile, I used to go and help an old chap named Sutton wash the tailing heaps of the mine for little diamonds that had been overlooked! He used to find little ones, but never gave me any. Once his Kaffirs found a good one about the size of a big pea in the bath (the thing they are turning, see sketch).

One day a man of the S.A.C., from Jacobsdal, turned up on foot, stripped; he had had a pretty bad time of it by his account.

He was evidently a very new hand at the business. He had lost his patrol about half-way between Jacobsdal and Koffyfontein, and though it was close to the river and he only had to follow the river to get to Jacobsdal about ten miles off, he wandered for two days without any food, till he saw a few Boers, to whom he promptly gave himself up, to get some food. There were two old men and two boys; the boys were very anxious to shoot him, but the old fellows would not, and sent him in to Koffyfontein. He seemed rather proud of his adventures, but I cannot imagine how he got lost.

The Kaffir scouts from Koffyfontein "got their own back" on

WASHING THE TAILING HEAPS

the Boers once (I think it was before my time there, though). About six of them were out without a white man, and four or five Boers, not seeing till too late that they were Kaffirs, came down to surrender. The Kaffirs took their rifles, and then shot the lot!

I must have been a curious-looking object going about Koffyfontein in my convalescent days. I only had my dilapidated old trekking clothes, and of course was as thin as a rake at first (you soon get fat after enteric, though), so that they were hanging round me in baggy folds. At last a batch of us were sent in with an empty convoy to Modder River station, *en route* for Kimberley. We stopped one night at Jacobsdal in the cottage hospital, a ripping house in the square, where they did us very well. We entrained at Modder River station, and reached Kimberley about 4 p.m., where we were met by a medical staff corporal and taken on a branch line to the big hospital by De Beers' big mine. They all told us we were going home at once! The last batch from Koffyfontein had gone home, and all enterics were going.

I was not sure whether I wanted to go or not; however, for some things I would have enjoyed a trip home, and all the others were very anxious to go, so we were pretty cheerful. They put us in a convalescent ward and rigged us out in the blue flannel sort of convict suit, and the nurses all were sure we were to be invalided. Next morning the ward doctor came round—"Oh,

CONVALESCENT

you're the Koffyfontein lot; I don't want to see you, you're for home!"

The rest of that day we were strolling about with the air of veterans who had served our country faithfully and were about to reap our reward. Already we saw ourselves the admired of all the recruits in the depot or provisional battalion, and went to bed to dream of furlough and cheap beer!

Next day the P.M.O. was to come to mark our boards "home," and we stood strictly to attention by our cots trying hard to conceal a complacent smirk, and look as if we would like to fight to the death but were really too delicate! He was a truculent-looking individual, and glared at us as if he could read "malingerer" on our faces; but we didn't mind, and as soon as he was out of the door we dived for our boards—looked—and then sat down silently till the nurse went out of the ward before we dared speak! Scrawled across each man's sheet, in an unnecessarily emphatic manner, was one word—"Duty!"

In the words of the song, *Surely there must be some mistake*! But there wasn't. Next day we drew our kits and filed out with a last lingering look at our nice beds with clean sheets, and the bottled stout and other luxuries that we had got accustomed to, and were marched, feeling like a chain-gang going to Siberia, over to the detail camp to start again on the old game dust and sand everywhere in fine weather, and water and mud in wet!

"Surely there must be some mistake!"

CHAPTER 18

Rejoining the Column

I had not been in the detail camp ten minutes when I decided it was no place for me, if I could get out. It was about the rottenest mob I'd ever struck. Details from every regiment—regular, irregular, and militia—you could imagine, and mostly arrant loafers, the scum of their respective corps, who had got away from the fighting line, and meant to stop away. The worst were some Welsh militia. Next morning I applied to the commandant to be sent back to my column, and was refused, as the Kimberley garrison was under strength; besides, Plumer was away in the Eastern Transvaal somewhere.

Of course, no one knew me, and a day or so after, when I was lying in my tent with my coat off, the orderly-sergeant came round, spotted me, and said, "Do you want a staff billet?" Of course I jumped at it, anything to get out of that gang; so he said, "All right! Go over and report at the Remount Depot to relieve Private So-and-so."

Well, I knew a full corporal could not relieve a private; however, I said nothing. Of course, with my coat off, he did not know I was a corporal, so as soon as he had gone, I rolled up my kit and humped it over to the remount camp about a mile away, and reported as ordered. As luck would have it, no one in authority spotted anything wrong, so I took over my duties, which were: One week to answer the telephone by day, and next week to sleep in the office in case the telephone bell went at night! About the softest billet I'd had since Garrison Sergeant-Major at Fort Camden! I got on very nicely there; we employees had a little mess of our own, and could go out in town whenever we were off duty.

I thought I was settled in life, or till the end of the war at any rate; but the third day an orderly came to the door and inquired for "Corporal Jackson, an Mounted Infantry bloke." It appeared that the sergent-major of the detail camp was anxious to interview me, so rolling up my kit again (I knew I wouldn't come back) I trailed over to the sergeant-major's quarters. "Here, aren't you a corporal?" he began.

"Yessir."

"Well, what the —— did you go and relieve a private for?"

I assumed a vacuously innocent expression and opined that I was told to.— No, I hadn't told the orderly-sergeant I was a private; in fact, I couldn't imagine how the mistake had occurred. However, he got back on me before I got clear of that camp. There was not an extra guard, picket, escort, or burial party, that "that Mounted Infantry fellow" was not on! I was there for about three weeks after that. I found that I had no chance of getting away unless I was specially applied for from my column, so I wrote to Sergeant-Major Weston to apply for me, and settled down to wait. I had no money; however, I became very friendly

A SOFT JOB

185

with a Yeomanry man, and we used to go out to the theatre, etc., together at his expense.

There was a canteen in camp, so there was a good deal of drunkenness with the militiamen, etc. One day I was on guard on the quarter-guard and had twenty-three prisoners. They were mostly drunk, and as I only had three men, and the guard-room was a bell-tent, it was pretty lively. I had four of the worst in handcuffs, but on going to inspect them once I found them all sitting round a big stone doing "Houdini, the handcuff king," bashing their handcuffs on the stone! One had his broken.

Another adventure occurred on a guard over by the remount depot, myself and three men again. This guard mounted at retreat and dismounted at reveille. After reveille, however, they generally used to stay there a couple of hours, so that the second and first reliefs got two hours more sleep; and after I had posted the last sentry, I turned in and went to sleep. I was awakened by a roar outside: "Sergeant of the Guard! Turn out that Guard!" so I kicked up the others, and we fell out of the tent—of course, we had our accoutrements—on and fell in.

When I had collected myself a bit, I discovered a more than usually malignant-looking Field Officer capering round on a polo pony, with his orderly behind, and no sentry. I immediately resigned myself to fate and a court-martial, and stood strictly to attention at the "shoulder" while the old man spread himself all over the occasion. He must have been an adjutant for a long time when he was younger, I think, by his handling of the subject, and the peculiarly vindictive, triumphant sort of grin of rage he had on. He talked for about ten minutes without repeating himself or missing a point, and disappeared in a cloud of dust and language, leaving us with a confused idea that a lyddite shell had hit somewhere close!!

I naturally began on the sentry then, but he was the only unmoved person, and said, "It's all right, that old ——'s drunk; reveille went half an hour ago! We were finished at reveille, so the old field officer, who must have been making a night of it, had no case at all. I reported myself as a prisoner when I got in, and

THE FIELD OFFICER LETS HIMSELF GO

the old beggar was sending up his evidence by orderly and telephone. I never said anything till the preliminary trial came on.
The camp commandant was much amused, and seemed rather
pleased. I expect the old major got chaffed about turning out a
guard that had been dismounted half an hour! Of course, they
could have had me for not dismounting at the right time, but
they let that go.

We had a grand wet week, when the whole camp was under
a foot of mud and water. One of the 7th New Zealanders was
in my tent. He used to live in a singlet and a pair of drawers and
paddle about with a shovel scraping the mud from round our
tent, which promptly ran back again. He was happy enough,
though.

At last I was sent for to the orderly room, and informed that
I had been applied for from the column if I wanted to go. There
was not much doubt about that, so I was told I could go next
day, as there was a batch of some militia going down as far as De
Aar, and a 5th Q.I.B. was to go with me to the column which
was somewhere in the Eastern Transvaal. They got a last hit at
me by putting me in charge of this mob who were going to
De Aar, so that I had to get their rations, warrants, etc., and was
responsible for them arriving safe at their unit.

When we got to De Aar their crowd (then about thirty of
them) was not there, and no one knew or cared anything about
them, so I found out the oldest soldier, gave him their warrants,
etc., and dismissed them with my blessing. I wonder if any of
them rejoined their corps—I've often pitied that oldest soldier.

Meanwhile, I and the Q.I.B., a Scotchman who had been in
some Highland regiment twenty years or so before, before he
went to Australia, proceeded on our travels to find the column
via Norval's Pont, Bloemfontein, Johannesburg, and Volksrust. I
had a sort of standing order for rations on the stations, and with
much forethought I drew rations at every station we stopped
at, so that when we got to Volksrust we had enough coffee, tea,
and sugar to last us for months on trek. We did not hurry ourselves much; when we came to a place we liked the look of we

stopped the night and jumped the next train; to all inquiries we only had to say "rejoining our column," and no one interfered with us—if we had been trying to get away from the column, it would have been very different.

At last, after a week or ten days, we arrived at Volksrust, and established ourselves in a tent by the station that did not seem to belong to anyone. Next day I made inquiries and found that Plumer was out Ermelo way, and that some of the Queenslanders were down at Newcastle drawing remounts. So after a day or two at Volksrust I thought I might as well draw a remount—it would not do to rejoin without a horse, if I had to steal one; so we entrained again through Langs Nek tunnel, under Majuba and down into Natal to Newcastle.

Here there were about fifty Q.I.B.'s camped by the remount depot, tents and everything complete as if they were there for good, so I reported to their officer and camped down, myself and Scotty, in a bivouac of his slung on a telegraph pole and a rifle. Here we passed Christmas and had a pretty good time-lots of fruit, and bathing in the river. The horses had not arrived, so we had nothing to do.

When I had been with the Bushmen about a week, and was beginning to fancy myself one of "the push," five *desperadoes* belonging to my company rolled up, two from prison and the remainder from God knows where! "Coffee" Oakford and Sims, two of the celebrities of the company, and my old friend Guyatt, who had just finished three months "hard" for refusing to work! He was cold shoer for the company. The sergeant-major of the bushmen evidently did not like their looks, for he handed them over to me and told me to consider myself a separate unit; so I moved them off a hundred yards or so, and pitched a bivouac with a telegraph pole again for a post, and there settled down to wait for the horses.

We had a very easy time for a week or so, bathing in the river and going out in town when we thought we would. "Coffee" Oakford and Sims, who were mates, broke the monotony by getting up a fight about something—probably gambling. It

A BATTLE OF NEWCASTLE

was a most bloody affair, and was hailed by the whole camp as a welcome diversion in the general dullness. Sims sprained his wrist in the sixth round or so, and was assured by "Coffee" that it was lucky for him, as if it had not happened he'd have broke his —— neck! However, that ended it for the time.

When the horses arrived they were all Australian, and we had a lot of fun with them. Guyatt was a born horseman; he was never so happy as when he was on a bad bucking horse, and used to sit them wonderfully well, too. "Coffee" fancied himself a bit, too, but he was a boasting, blustering sort of chap—"the horse wasn't foaled that could chuck him," etc.

To do him justice, he would generally try to ride anything, however bad, but he got slung occasionally. He drew a very nice-looking little mare, and though she was a bit fresh she didn't do much; so "Coffee" was in great form, flying about the camp making her show herself, and got so confident that she was quiet that he rode her down to water bare-backed. (We generally used to put the saddle on till we knew our horses.)

About half-way to water an orderly galloping by or something startled the mare, and she set to work in a business-like manner. Coffee "came" at about the third buck! However, he got on again and quieted her. Guyatt was riding rough horses for anyone who would let him; and altogether, as the 5th Q.I.B. were not much of a bushmen corps, being recruited mostly from

GUYATT IN HIS GLORY

the towns, and as there were only five of us, we kept up quite a reputation for horsemanship. I was afraid at first that we were going to look rather foolish with the whalers amongst the Australians; but I only saw one man there who could ride, and he could. Mitchell was his name, "Walley" Mitchell; he could ride anything you could show him, and he used to break all the bad horses for the others. He and Guyatt did a great competition business, but Mitchell never got put off, and Guyatt thought he wasn't getting his money's worth if he wasn't!

I drew a big raw-boned animal that the bushmen, by way of cheering me up, said looked like a bad 'un all over. Walley, who was rather a friend of mine, offered to try him first; but I didn't like to be shown up by Guyatt and "Coffee," so I took him out to where they had thrown the dung from all the horse lines, for I thought it would be soft falling, and mounted gingerly with an expectant audience. Much to my relief, and the disgust of the rest, the old chap walked off like a lamb.

Another party from my company came down for remounts, and I heard the news from the column that three of my company had been killed since I left them, in an affair at a farm in the Free State. They had surrounded the place in the night, and at daybreak were rushing it when a sergeant and two men were shot dead. They had supposed me to be dead, as I had been reported a hopeless case. (This must have been when I was having

AN ANXIOUS MOMENT "WILL HE BUCK?"

a glorious time living—on champagne and brandy). However, I soon convinced them that, barring a swollen ankle, I was as good as new.

Myself and my five being now mounted, we were packed off with a party of Q.I.B. for Volksrust *en route* for the column. We stayed at Volksrust a few days, as the column was trekking and was not expected at Wakkerstroom (a day's march from Volksrust) for a week or so. Here we heard of the Yeomanry smash-up at Tweefontein.

There was a canteen open from 12 noon to 1 p.m., each man only allowed one canteenfull. We had to line up and get it. You'd see a beery old soldier or a flash bushman draw his pint and drink it off and run round to the tail of the procession to take his turn for another. I used to sympathise with the N.C.O. on canteen duty; but it was generally a whiskery old veteran of a sergeant, who was well able to run things.

Rather an amusing thing occurred here. The officer of the Bushmen, a very young fellow and not a bad sort at all, lost a lot of his kit, and, on searching through the kits of his gallant command (thirty bushmen and myself and commando, "Coffee" Sims, etc.), he found some of it in the bundle of one of the "bushies," so naturally made him a prisoner for theft. However, in a day or two's time, when we were to trek, the remainder of the bushmen refused to go without the prisoner! So he was released, and everyone was satisfied except, I suppose, the little officer.

"WALLEY" MITCHELL QUIETING AN OUTLAW

"Beating the double attack"

CHAPTER 19

The Death of
Sergeant-Major Weston

We were all ready to start now, and were only waiting for definite news of the column, when a convoy came in from Wakkerstroom, about fourteen miles east from Volksrust, and with it a lot of Plumer's wounded; and we got some bad news from them. We were hanging about our camp, having picketed and fed our horses for the night, when some bushmen came up who had escorted the convoy in, and I went over to hear the news from the column. Plumer had had a pretty stiff fight out Ermelo way with Louis Botha.

Major Valentine was killed, and a lot of yeomanry, bushmen, etc. "Your company got it worst," the man said to me. "Your captain, sergeant-major, any amount of non-coms., and a quarter of your men!" I was pretty anxious to know who were killed, as of course I had a lot of friends in the company, so was glad we marched next morning for Wakkerstroom, where the column was lying.

We reached Wakkerstroom about mid-day, and could not see the column, so halted in the town; and a terrific hailstorm came on. We had a lively quarter hour—hailstones as big as pigeon's eggs—they hurt like blazes, and we had no cover, or couldn't take it as we had to hold the horses, which were driven frantic. We crouched down with a horse blanket over our heads and the hailstones barking our knuckles, which were uncovered holding the reins.

When this was over I heard that most of our wounded were in a house in town, so I went off to see them. I got permission from the doctor, and was shown into one room where poor old Weston was. I had last seen him when he came to look me up in hospital at Koffyfontein. He was looking very well and jolly, said he thought I was dead! and gave me an account of the fight which I may as well give now:—

The column had halted for mid-day in some of the old, undulating ridge and furrow sort of country, and had off-saddled, etc., when a few Boers appeared on the top of a neighbouring ridge and began sniping. Plumer sent a party—bushmen, I think—to clear them off, and this party, instead of just clearing the ridge and holding it, kept following these few snipers from ridge to ridge (they had a pom-pom with them), till suddenly, from a convenient *donga*, emerges Louis Botha and the whole firm!

Our side had just time to get to some sort of cover with the pom-pom, and presumably to get a man away for reinforcements, before they were cut off. Meanwhile, the troops in camp were grazing their horses and having lunch, when Plumer sent over to our company to go and relieve these men; so off they went, I have no doubt, cursing the bushmen for getting cornered in the heat of the day. When they got up most of them joined the other party, but Captain Leigh, the sergeant-major, and a section went off to an exposed ridge on a flank, which wanted holding for some reason. Major Valentine and staff and four or five bushmen joined them here, and this was where the slaughter took place.

The firing-line were lying on the ridge with no cover and their horses just down in the hollow behind them. Louis Botha himself was heading the attack at this point, and rushed his men up at the gallop to within fifty yards, when they dismounted leaving their horses, and took what cover they could get. There was a heavy fire kept upon both sides for some time. Pretty deadly, too; almost all the hits were in the head. Captain Leigh was hit in the neck and thigh, and had a bullet in the stock of his carbine, and his field-glasses smashed.

Sergeant-Major Weston, raising himself on his hands and knees to get a sight on a Boer, was hit by a bullet coming over his shoulder, striking his bandolier on his back and bursting two or three cartridges. Major Valentine was shot dead, and his orderly wounded. After a time our men could hear Botha urging his men to rush, but they would not for a long time, and they could hear the *veldt* cornets' "Kom, kom, ye must kom."

At last, after they had wormed themselves up to about twenty yards off, they did come, and a lot were shot coming, as in many cases the fellows did not stop firing till they had two or three rifles held to their heads. Meanwhile all the remainder had retired and, owing to this section's resistance, had got the pom-pom away as well; so Botha, after a look round, saw he was too late, and after a short talk with Captain Leigh, cleared off in a hurry, as he thought the column would be coming up soon. He took all the unwounded men to bury his dead (this was a favourite game of theirs), letting them go afterwards.

Botha allowed no looting; he only asked Captain Leigh for his field-glasses, and was much amused when he found they were smashed by one of his bullets. The burial party he took found he had more dead than we had. Of course, he got all his wounded away, but seeing he did not get any ammunition (ours being all fired, bar a few odd rounds) and took very few rifles (a lot of the men threw their rifles away in the long grass when they found the Boers on top of them, and they had no time to look for them), Botha lost a good deal more than he gained. However, when ours came to take stock they found not much to laugh about.

There had only been about thirty or forty altogether, and of them Major Valentine was killed, Captain Leigh very badly wounded, Sergeant-Major Weston mortally wounded, a sergeant and corporal killed, and I don't know how many men. A draft had joined while I was away, so I did not know the men killed, except about eight, most of them good old hands, who had been trekking all the time since the start. Nearly all were hit through the head, some two or three times.

One very decent chap was hit twice, and remarked, "Well, I've got it twice; that's enough at a time," and began to crawl back over the slope when he got it again, which finished him. This was up in the firing-line; but the horse-holders got it worst: they were down in a slight hollow behind, and when the Boers rushed they came round on both sides of them. Tilbury, that corporal who had been doing sergeant-major for the yeomanry-the same man that went with me to reconnoitre Broadwood's camp—was in charge of led horses; he had only just come back from the yeomanry to take sergeant in the company, and little Dick Dale (the man who was always getting the shells round him) was with him, and of course several more.

They could have got away, but would not go as long as there was a chance of the men in front wanting the horses, and the Boers came round and shot them all point blank, most of them through the head. Evidently Botha's presence had restrained them on the ridge, as they did no shooting in cold blood up there. Kipling is *talking through his hat* in his poem *Mounted Infantry*, when he makes out No. 3's (horse-holders') to have an easy safe time. It's the most trying business of the lot.

Imagine on a small patrol in bad country, about five of you being left at the bottom of a great rambling *kopje* with eighteen horses, while the remainder go away out of sight up the *kopje*, and you can hear them getting heavily engaged. You don't know what they are doing or how they are getting on, and you do know that the first you'll hear of them being captured or cut off will be a volley at yourself from the nearest ridge of the *kopje*.

Besides, you might be taken on the flanks or rear yourself. I know I always preferred the firing-line, and felt safer there, too. Then, again, in open country you are just behind the firing-line, and as the Boers cannot see the firing-line lying down they fire at the horses. The only man of the section who got away was a regular old country yokel, who was leading the ammunition mule, and he rode straight through the Boers. They must have taken him for one of themselves!

After wishing Weston a good trip home, I went and saw Captain Leigh, and was sorry to find him looking very bad indeed. I thought it was a case of days with him, hit as he was in almost the same place as Major Welch had been, and with other wounds as well. However, he evidently did not think things were so bad as they looked, and gave me several instructions for the officer in charge of the company, re pay, etc., and took the trouble to give me minute instructions about getting a commission in S.H.C., which he knew I had been trying for, which to say the least of it was more than most would have done.

We found the column eventually about four miles out, and the company were much surprised to see me, as they had thought me dead; and I fell 60 *per cent,* in the estimation of the "fly" set for having enteric badly, and not knowing enough to "work it" home! We stopped in this camp under Graskop for about a week; the outposts had the worst of it, as they were down in a *vlei,* all green dank grass and rushes up to the waist, and the mosquitoes were very bad. My old black mare was in the company still, belonging to a man in charge of the water-cart, so she had a pretty easy time.

In about three days' time we got the news of Weston's death; we were very much surprised, for we had not thought it very serious; but mortification set in, and he died at Charlestown. I was very sorry; we had always been very good friends from the time I was in his room as a recruit at Birr. (He was corporal then, and very popular.) Captain Leigh had horrified the hospital staff by insisting on attending the funeral, against the doctor's orders. He was invalided home, and got all right again, I am glad to say. I think he is in India now, but I bet he will not forget the 7th Mounted Infantry in a hurry.

Most of them will remember him, anyway. He was pretty well known. If anything annoyed him you could hear his remarks at the other end of the column; but it was all over in a minute, and he would be chattering to the non-com, he had just been slating as if nothing had happened. He was the terror of the

"LED NOT DRIVEN"

cockney recruits we used to get from the battalion. I remember once a man turned out with a straggly, scrubby-looking beard. Now Captain Leigh ("Buster" was his nickname) always liked us to keep as soldierly as possible, and made us wear helmets and everything regimental, though he was not foolishly strict on trek; so when he came on parade on this occasion, and came to the man with the whiskers, he stopped and glared at him for about a minute, with his face getting redder and redder. Then his eyes began to roll, and out it came in a bellow: "Damn you! go and shave!! I'm the only Bashibazouk in this crowd!!!" (He always wore a beard himself). I don't know whether he got a D.S.O. or anything; he ought to have; he saved a gun on two separate occasions.

It was rotten bad country all round Wakkerstroom, so I was disgusted to find myself told off for advanced screen the first day we trekked; and we had not gone six miles before my forebodings were realised! I had got on to a low rise facing a nasty looking *nek*, when an orderly came up to tell me the column was halted, and I was to stop where I was. So I got the horses down in a *kraal* and spread my commando along the ridge, not troubling much about cover, as we could see round for more than rifle range.

Presently, I noticed about eight mounted men coming up from about the direction I thought the column was in, as the road we had come had been bearing round to the right a lot.

CAPTAIN LEIGH PARALYSING ONE OF THE "LARST DRAFT".

About four of us were sitting together talking, when these eight men dismounted behind a few rocks about 400 yards off. This made me pretty sure they were a Cossack post from the column, so that we got rather a jar when they emptied their magazines at us and then cleared at the gallop. They were jolly close, too, but we "stood not upon the order of our going" over the dip, at the first discharge, and no one was hit.

We halted at a little place called Amersfoort, at a ripping farm, where they said Rider Haggard had written one of his books. We did a lot of night-work at this time, camping in the daytime, and the whole mob going off at night and taking up positions on *kopjes* and drifts, etc. The man who took our half column, in Valentine's place, was the commanding officer of the Bushmen, a Major Vyalls, universally known as "Biltong." He had a very good name, but I can only answer for his being a capable whiskey drinker!

He used to carry a flask with him, and have a good eye-opener at every halt. I believe he was a good man, but he never got much chance of proving it while I knew him. He affected the bluff, blustering manner. When he took us over he paraded us all—the yeomanry, bushmen, and ourselves—to give us a speech, and jumped on an officer who was getting his company into position, telling him he was not in the cavalry now! So the officer stopped giving orders, and told his men to get round, and they were straggling out of the ranks and got round old Biltong like schoolchildren round their mistress. I thought Biltong looked the more foolish of the two.

One night we were going on a long night march, and I had no horse; mine had gone wrong before we left Wakkerstroom, and I was riding spare ones. This day I saw a nice-looking horse loose in the lines. He was a bushman's, and I knew they were not going on this game; so I collared him and we started just before dusk, and marched out straight through the bushmen's lines! Of course they twigged him, and I had to give him up and dismount one of my section to get a horse. (I was in charge of a section).

"We stood not upon the order of our going"

We went to the Assegai River that night, and held a *drift* that they thought Botha was making for, but he did not come. Going down a mountainside an old Kaffir woman was standing at her *kraal kow-towing* to everyone that passed, much to the amusement of the cockney recruits. The old girl was saying *N'kose, N'kose* (chief), to everyone, and Van-der-Steyn or one of them exclaimed—"In course, my good woman, in course," and waved his hand in a benedictory way. The old girl was quite pleased.

The cockneys were great on the Kaffir language. They'd ride up to a *kraal* and ask for eggs or something, and the woman would say "*Ikona*" (no). "*Ide park corner*," says 'Enery, "blowed if I didn't think I'd seen you at St. James' 'All!"

About this time a new regiment of Mounted Infantry came out and joined Plumer, and we were drafted on to them, much to our disgust. We had had a good time on our own, no one to worry us but our captain, and we didn't like going back to the adjutants, regimental sergeant-majors, etc., of a full regiment; besides, the commanding-officer, a Major "Gogaty," was a bit of a martinet, and went in for the cast-iron sort of discipline that we had dropped two years before and had got out of the way of. And there was a good deal of trouble with our fellows and the Buff company of the 5th Mounted Infantry who had joined him, too.

We didn't like exchanging the old 7th Mounted Infantry for the 27th. The 27th was about the last Mounted Infantry, and it made us wild on going into the line, or touching other columns, to see the superior airs put on by corps (even yeomanry) who had been longer in the field than the 27th, but had not been formed when we had been trekking for a year! Served us right, I suppose, for the airs we had put on in the 7th! Not having a horse of my own, and being in charge of a section, I used to have a pretty good time, as I'd dismount any of my men with a good horse and take it.

The men didn't mind a soft day with the wagons. I got sold once, though—I noticed a man in my section who would not keep in the ranks, and on checking him he said he could not

Van der Steyn and the Kaffir woman

hold his horse, so as I did not care much for the one I was riding, I changed with him, and was soon very sorry for it. It was on a night march, and this pony had a mouth like a brick, and the more you pulled the faster he went. I pulled till his head was round to my knee, and then he started trotting, and if you kept on pulling he'd break into a canter, and so on.

Most curious animal! He took me right up in front of the column two or three times. I rode him next day, and my fingers were stiff with cramp and blistered; I got him changed next time we went to Wakkerstroom. I got the third stripe about this time, so moved from the horse-lines to the sergeants' mess, which luxurious establishment was situated at the end of the lines under a wagon!

It was a great thing having your supper ready cooked for you when you got into camp at night; the wagons generally got in long before the mounted troops, who would be away on the flanks and different guards—advance, rear, or flank. The old wagon man, "Dad" Blatchford, used to cook for us, so everything was ready when we off-saddled, instead of our having to make a fire (in the rain perhaps) and cook as well, as we had to do in the lines.

The sergeant's mess

CHAPTER 20

With Kitchener

We worked for some time all along the Ermelo-Wakker-stroom block-house line, round the Slangaped Mount (I'm not sure if that's spelt right) and the Pongolo Bush, across to Stand-erton. Once we went off for a night manoeuvre near Graskop. An officer and myself and section were left behind a bit as rear-guard; it was very dark, so we could not keep far behind. We saw the column halt in front; we could just distinguish a black mass on the slope of a rise, so we halted in the valley. We'd been there a long time, when the officer got nervous and sent me on to see why they were waiting so long; and I discovered that the black mass was a Kaffir *kraal*.

There were no signs of the main body. I reported, and the officer told me to gallop on and see if I could find them, and he'd come along the road cautiously. I caught up the column about five miles ahead, and went back; we were coming on at the trot, when suddenly we made out a body of mounted men on our left rear, coming up pretty quick! We took up a position in a dry *spruit* and waited; presently they came over the rise and down the road at a smart canter. Most exciting! We were just going to let rip when the officer told me to challenge, just as a matter of form; and it was lucky I did, for they were a party of our own who'd been searching a farm.

That night we took up a position all along a very rocky *kopje*. In the morning there was a dense fog, but when it cleared off we had a fine sight—there was a great valley below us, all ravines and *donga*s, very rough country; and on all the hills round the sort of amphitheatre we could make out troops, and a body of men were just going in to draw through the valley!

As we watched we could see them putting up convoys of Boers at every farm, till there were about sixty running round like a rat in a trap, getting fired at from every lot of troops they came near, looking for an opening; finally, they all got together in a body, and galloped off towards the block-house line. We thought we were going to see some sport if they broke through, but they surrendered to a block-house, and we went home. We went off to within sight of Ermelo then, and did a night march towards Standerton.

The following night I was having supper in the "mess" when an order came down to Murdoch to find a section for duty with Toll's column that night, and he promptly detailed me, much to my disgust. I saddled up and got my section over to where Toll was formed up, and reported. No one knew anything about me and cared less, so I made a separate unit of myself and section and trekked along with the column on my own all night. In the morning we were within sight of Standerton, and thirty or forty Boers were caught between us and the line, and an armoured train started firing at them; so they surrendered to us while they were safe! We all camped down then, I still on my own (I don't know what they had wanted us for at all), and took it easy all day till the remainder of the column came up.

We stopped at Standerton a day or two, and Plumer left us and went home; then we trekked west of the line (a night-march, of course). French, now sergeant, got thrown and sprained his ankle, so got six weeks' rest. We made a half circle round to Volk-srust, nearly getting into the Free State. We were burning a lot of farms; most of them had ammunition hidden in the thatch, and *feu de joies* were going off all round. It was very broken country—all *donga*s and ravines.

One day we were riding along in one little valley, when a most terrific fire broke out in the next valley. We made sure that the troops there were getting rushed in force, and galloped over the rise at best pace; but it was only the bushmen, who had come suddenly on a herd of spring-buck and were doing independent firing at them. It was like old times to see spring-buck again; we hadn't seen them since we left the Eastern Free State.

Next day we had marched through several nasty rocky passes in some *krantzes*, and were halted in the plain beyond, waiting for the convoy to come up, when our captain got an order to take a couple of sections back after the convoy, as a few Boers were hanging round. So back we went through the passes again till we came to where we had been told the convoy was. No sign of them. It seems they had taken another road round. I did not much like the situation; it was horrible country—great ravines leading up to us from all sides, and steep *donga*s that you could put a regiment into.

For some reason or other the captain kept hanging about, and I was watching the *donga*s and *kopjes* all round; presently, just as I expected, about twelve rode over a rise about 800 yards off, and had come some distance towards us before they saw us. When they did, they went back behind some rocks and watched us, and then we could see twos and threes all about watching us. I began to feel like a chicken, with a hawk in the sky, for they could have surrounded us easily; however, at last we went, going round by the road the column had taken.

On the way we saw a man in the distance, riding a horse and leading another. The captain wanted a man to go and see who it was, and as I felt tolerably sure it was someone belonging to the column, I volunteered and cantered over to him. When I got about 200 yards from him he dismounted and went behind his horse! I made sure he was going to shoot, and cursed myself for not sending someone else; however, he didn't, and I found it was only an unarmed Kaffir—probably a Boer scout—and I let him go.

On the following day we were right flank-guard over very bad ground again, and we saw plenty of signs of Boers. At one farm we had just run in a mare and foal and caught the mare; when we got to the farmhouse it was deserted, but a horse was standing in the stable, saddled and bridled, and in a lather of sweat; he had been shot in the leg. The column halted about a mile beyond this. We had searched the gardens and everywhere, but could not find the rider of the white horse.

From where we halted we could see the rear-guard in this farm searching for loot. I suppose, anyway, they must have been very careless, for we suddenly saw about forty Boers come over the rise at the gallop—they had evidently been watching—and make down for the farm. You can imagine that it was pretty exciting for us, for we didn't know if our chaps could see them; and as it turned out, they had not, for the Boers were going strong about 300 yards from the house before we saw our chaps running about the farm buildings, getting their horses under cover, etc.

Then they opened fire from the *kraal*, and drove the Boers back to the top of the rise, where they stopped and fired into the farm. It must have been getting too warm, as the rear-guard after a time left the farm and went on to a *kopje* close by. And then for some reason or other the captain took us back at the gallop, right past the rear-guard and after the Boers, who had retired to lure us on, evidently thinking they had a "soft thing" on. However, after going about a mile and a half past the rear-guard, we fired a few rounds at them, and retired like a terrier that has been barking at a bicycle! I thought it was a good thing the column commander could not see how we had left his right flank exposed.

We passed a farm that they said was old Joubert's, and camped close to Volksrust. When we moved in to Volksrust we heard about Methuen's big smash-up, and we could tell that something was up by the stir in the town—staff officers flying about, troops going up through in the train, and more troops collecting at Volksrust. We soon found out that we were to go round to the Western Transvaal to take part in the big movement against De La Rey; and in a day or two we entrained, bag and baggage, and set off *via* Johannesburg. Near Heidelberg I recognised with affection a nice, solid, stone culvert that had afforded me excellent cover for a long time in the fight when Ian Hamilton broke his shoulder.

It rained all the time to Johannesburg, and we were crowded in open trucks; everything hollow collected pools of water, and waited for a jolt of the train to empty it down your neck, or into your boot. Then, by way of rubbing it in, they steamed slow through Park Station, Johannesburg, past the buffet and dining room, about 8 o'clock in the evening, so that we could see them having a glorious spread in a brilliantly lighted saloon—officers in good uniforms, theatre parties, ladies in evening dress, etc.- and we went so slow that we could see the different courses being brought to different tables.

Several got so excited over the scene that they wished to bombard the plate-glass windows with bully-beef tins and biscuits, but were dissuaded on the grounds that we were expecting a big pay day at Klerksdorp (every man was about 60 in credit), and would certainly have to pay for the damage. There was a slight collision in Johannesburg, but only a horse-box was smashed up.

We went straight on down the Klerksdorp line. It is a desolate looking country after you pass the mines on the Rand, and we had a monotonous journey. It took us till late the following day to reach Klerksdorp, but here things were a bit more cheerful. The little one-horse town and station was alive with troops just arrived and arriving, and we had to take possession of the first bit of bare ground we could see for our horse-lines, where we waited for the second train-load, which arrived next morning.

Then we marched out through the town, past a *kopje*, and on to a plain the other side. Here was the camp where the punitive force was mobilising. And there was a crowd! The whole place was covered with camps—seven or eight columns, I should think—with only a roadway left between them. Nearly all were mounted men; so the veldt was black with horse-lines and mobs out grazing.

The following are some of the columns: Kitchener, Thornycroft, Keir, Cookson, Lowe, Rawlinson—and those are not all.

We did nothing for a day or two. Our camp was down by the river, and we grazed the horses; they wanted it, as they had had some hard trekking in the Eastern Transvaal, and the railway journey had not improved their legs. I had a Canadian mare—a good one.

At this time De La Key's headquarters were at Hartebeeste-fontein, a little village about eight miles out of Klerksdorp, and his outposts were in the Klerksdorp gold mines, about two miles from our camp. We could see them riding about, and there was a lot of sniping between them and our outposts, who were on a green ridge.

One day there was a bit of excitement. Some Kaffir scouts of ours went out to a farm about a mile from us, and one of them got caught. We heard a shot. When we moved out a day or two after I happened to pass the place, and I was riding along, not thinking of anything in particular, when suddenly in the long grass I saw a dead horse; he had a saddle on, so I went up to him, and there was the Kaffir lying by his head—dead, of course.

At last Kitchener drew up his scheme, and one day every man was paraded to hear orders, which were to this effect: There was to be a night march that night. Only the good horses were to go. (A good horse meant in that case a horse that might crawl fifty or sixty miles, even if he died as soon as he had done it.) As we were going a long way, and going quick, we were to understand that any man whose horse gave out would be left, and must look out for himself; and he wouldn't have much chance, for we were going straight through the Boers' positions.

As we were likely to get scattered during the night, we wore white bands round our helmets, so that we should know our side, *à la Huguenot*. We were going to drive back extended for about forty miles, and nab De La Rey between us and the line, which was lined with infantry. I think it would be a good plan if they always gave out what they were trying to do, as naturally men don't take much interest in what they know nothing about. There would have been much more dash in the operations as a rule, but I suppose they were afraid of the plans getting known by the Boers.

Well, this night we started about dusk, all the mounted troops moving out in different directions. We went slightly south-west from Klerksdorp, leaving the mines on our right. My mare was very puffy about the forelegs from the journey in the truck, and limped a bit; but I thought it would wear off, and anyway, she was fitter than a lot more that had to go. As soon as we got clear of camp we could hear them drawing out in front, and we trotted for about three miles, then walked for twenty minutes, and off again, and so on all night.

About midnight we were trotting through a thick patch of bush, and just as we pulled up for a walk I noticed two men on our flank who did not belong to us, so I rode out to them. One waited, and the other cantered on for fifty yards or so. I asked this chap if he was looking for the I.L.H., like a fool; I could see he was not a regular, and as he was in khaki I took it for granted he was an irregular. He, of course, said Yes, and I showed him where they were in front. As I was riding back to the company I happened to look round and saw my two friends just disappearing in the bush straight out to our right, and there were no troops that way. I wondered then if they were Boers, and it turned out afterwards that they must have been. We heard later that odd Boers were riding with us all that night!

Soon after that we came to a farm under a white limestone *kopje*, and here we halted for about ten minutes. Several of my section came to me with very long faces; their horses were getting done up. All I could do for them was to tell them which I thought was the nearest way home! My old mare was going very lame when she trotted, and I was not at all sure that she would last out; but she was game enough, and gave no signs of being tired. (We had come about twenty miles by this time, trotting most of the way.)

When we started again the poor old crocks had got stiff, and had started falling out, especially the big-boned old Hungarians. I couldn't help laughing sometimes at some of the old wrecks that dropped back past us from the front companies; the expressions of lively anxiety on the men's faces would have been very funny if one could have been sure that the Boers, who were certain to bail them up, would not shoot first and ask questions afterwards. It is never pleasant to see a beaten horse punished, but under the circumstances you could not blame the men, and there was great execution done with the buckle ends of baggage straps, etc.

DONE UP

Chapter 21

"Drives"

There were a lot of curious little adventures amongst those who fell out. There were about five in our company, and I may as well give their adventures now, though we didn't hear them till, in some cases, weeks afterwards! Lance-Corporal Russell, that chap who had been one of the five when old Pile got hit, was well mounted (a good man always was); but soon after the halt—about 1 a.m., I suppose—his pony fell in an ant-bear hole. When Russell (in common with all short men in the army, he answered to the nickname of "Stump") collected himself, he was just in time to see the troops disappearing in the darkness—we were trotting at the time—and his pony galloping after them! He knew it was nearly thirty miles back to Klerksdorp, and thought we might halt soon, so walked on after us. Presently a Kaffir rode up from behind him on a mule, looked at him and went back.

Of course, "Stump" was not such a fool as to shoot, so he hid his rifle in the long grass, and sat on an ant-heap. Presently three or four Boers rode up and held him up; they stripped him clean, and gave him an old horse blanket. We picked him up next day on our way back, as cool as ever. We had his horse, so he only lost his clothes, which was a good thing for him, for of course they rigged him out fresh when we got back to Klerksdorp.

It used to be great fun picking up a man who had been stripped like that; his expressions were so funny as the troops came up to him, and you can imagine the chaff a wretched man had to stand as a column rode past him, with perhaps nothing but a torn shirt and a pair of No. 14 Boer *veldt-shoen* on! They did not get much change out of Russell, though; he took it in a very matter-of-fact way.

Another man named Sharpe fell out in the wood where I saw the two Boers, and as soon as he was left he was amongst the Boers. They were riding just behind us. We had passed within 300 yards of their *laager*, where they had three or four guns! He said they were in rather a stew—didn't know where to go-so kept following us to see where we were going. They took Sharpe's horse and made him ride on a gun-carriage, so he got a beautiful view of the proceedings.

As I say, they followed us all night; and at daybreak, when we had got as far as we were going, and were extending to meet the columns on either side to drive back to the line, they dodged through some hilly country between our column and the next. Probably we saw them and took them for our side. Sharpe said it was a near thing several times; they would come round a hillock almost on to a company of ours, and dodge back and round the other side; and once they sat their horses in a clump in a steep hollow, expecting every moment to see our helmets over the rise, as they had seen a mob coming straight for them, but they went into the next *kloof*.

Of course, Sharpe was given to understand that to make any sign would not be healthy for him. They kept him a fortnight or so, and treated him pretty well.

Two more, a fellow named Wing and another, got left soon after the halt. The other fellow went back, and he was about the only man of the column who reached Klerksdorp complete-horse, rifle, etc. Wing waited till morning, when he was captured, stripped, and started off on his own. He lost his bearings and went due south instead of east. At a farm he got a feed from a Dutch woman, and soon after found a horse, which he appropriated; but he had not gone far, when some Boers caught him up, and had a heated discussion as to the advisability of shooting him for theft! However, they let him off, and he reached the Vaal block-house line, where he stayed for about a month.

To return to ourselves. We went on in the same way till just on daybreak, when we began to get some sport. First we came on an outpost all asleep—about seven of them! We gathered them in before they were properly awake, and soon after struck a small *laager* by a farm. It gave me rather a shock. I was jogging along more than half asleep in the grey, misty sort of half-light, when I suddenly found myself amongst a lot of wagons, looking blurred and indistinct, with white, ghost-like faces peering out at us, and our commanding-officer talking in stage whispers: "Thanks, just come out of those wagons."

"Any rifles?"

"Thank you; Sergeant-Major, tell off an escort for these prisoners," and we had gone on into the mist before I was quite sure I hadn't dreamt it all. Then we struck a single sentry fast asleep behind an ant-heap. I remember thinking how cold he must have been, for there was a bitter wind blowing, as he stood up in his shirt and trousers and rolled up his blanket.

He looked upon the affair as rather a joke, and smiled at us in a most friendly way, as much as to say: "Good! I didn't think you had it in you!" Then just over the rise from him we came on quite a respectable *laager*—twenty wagons or more, a lot of women, sheep, cattle, and quite a nice little lot of prisoners. It was while we were getting them fixed up that Sharpe's chums were breaking through.

This was as far as we were going, and we spread out to join the columns on either side; and without a halt for feed for ourselves or horses, drove back the way we had come, getting back to Hartebeestefontein that night, picking up "Stump" Russell on the way, and altogether about sixty prisoners. I think our column (Lowe's) only got about seven coming back. Eighty-three miles they said we had done, and I should think it must have been all that; I know I was pretty sick of it before we camped. The mare had stood it splendidly; she got over the lameness before we got to the *laager*.

It only just missed being an important capture, as the mob

with the guns only got through by pure luck. Two of our prisoners were recognised by the I.L.H. as deserters, and next day they had a sort of court-martial on them. We thought they would be shot, but they sent them into Klerksdorp, and I don't know what became of them.

This was a great *mealie* country. You could see great patches of *mealies* (maize) all over the place, and for two or three weeks we did nothing but pick cobs—quite a *harvest home* affair. The column used to camp at a convenient place, and we would go out by companies with wagons, past outposts, and get to work filling the wagons with the ripe cobs. All the animals had as many as they would eat, and the remainder we used to send in to the line. I got very sick of *mealie* picking; but occasionally you'd strike a melon-patch, and your fatigue party would miss you for a time!

About a fortnight after the big night-march, we were about two days' trek[1] out from Klerksdorp, on the line of the night-march. We were going to camp in a valley between two bare rises, with a rushy swamp of a stream running through. I was told off for look-out post as soon as we got there; and when we got out about 800 yards and had off-saddled, the sentry walking about came on a dead body; so I sent in to report, and a party came out to bury him. We heard then that they had found fifteen more in camp!—all I.L.H. men (Imperial Light Horse, a Johannesburg corps). They had been cut off on the night, I think.

We were with both Keir's and Cookson's columns at this time, and I nearly got into that fight they had. I had been away to see a body some other corps had found to see if it was Wing, who had not turned up at that time—and was riding along with the convoy, taking my time about rejoining the company, when on looking behind I saw that one lot was camping. I made inquiries, and found it was my column, so went back, Keir and Cookson going on. That night there was a great commotion.

About thirty men, Canadians and Mounted Infantry, turned up in a tremendous hurry—some bare-backed—with news that

---

1. Ordinary treks

Keir's and Cookson's columns had been heavily attacked. They had been cut off while watering horses. (They were put back for a court-martial for coming away; I don't know if they cleared themselves.)

Apparently Lowe did not think it was pressing, for we did not move till morning, when we struck out through some very thick bush. I was on advance-guard, and did not much like my job, as, besides the bush, there were a lot of *mealie* patches with *mealies* about ten feet high, and we knew the place was infested with Boers.

At last we came to a farm with some wounded Boers in it, and I suppose they told us the way to Cookson's *laager*, for we turned off sharp to the left; and after trekking some time through bush, we came out on the edge of the open country. About a mile and a half in front was a reedy *sluit* with a farm on it, and another one a quarter of a mile from it. A crowd was round the first farm, and they were watching us, evidently suspecting that we were old Delarey coming back. However, a helio on the roof got communication with us, and we went down.

There had been pretty hard fighting. The place was littered with dead horses, both Boer and British—you could tell the difference by the saddles as a rule. They had collected the dead and wounded, and were straightening things up. The fighting had been hottest round the second farm. I think the Canadians did well; they were rushed several times, but held them off with the bayonet. We all went back to Dreikuil, our camp. The dead horses (Boers') were very thick in the long grass on a rise opposite the little farm. We passed a farm where Delarey had left some of his wounded.

We kept this camp on Dreikuil for a week or so, going out for long patrols every day through the bush. We had a night attack here. We had been expecting them for some time, and had shanties built of stone (the camp was on a hill). This night we had had supper and were playing cards in the tent (the sergeant's mess had risen to a bell-tent now), when there was a sudden sputter of shots from the outpost. We tumbled out and dug out our sections from their bivouacs and blankets, and went out to the outpost line. The machine-gun was going under forced draft, but it soon blew over and we turned in.

Next, we started off south on a drive. On these drives we were extended in a single unbroken line, about fifty yards between files, and the end file of one column touching the end of the next, so that we covered forty or fifty miles; then we'd go ahead with a section every here and there behind the line as supports, and the guns and convoy blocking up behind. At night we slept where we stopped, and as we used to drive on to a block-house line and let the flanks get a little ahead, any Boers in that district had to fight or surrender.

Delarey had a name for fighting, so you can imagine my joy when, about the third day out, I emerged from a belt of timber, with no one in sight but a file or two stretching away into the scrub on each side of me, and beheld sixty odd Boers on the opposite rise about 600 yards off, scattered about, all mounted and looking at me! I withdrew as unassumingly as possible back into the timber, and sent a report back to the officer. But before reinforcements came the commando cantered off over the rise, going half-right towards Kekewich's column. When we moved on I passed their camp, half down by a reed bed and half round a farmhouse.

We went on for a day or two longer, through some bush where the locusts were so thick that they had broken big limbs off the trees where they had settled. Then we heard that the mob I had seen had broken through Kekewich the same afternoon. De Wet heads one of his chapters very grandiloquently: *I cut my way through sixty thousand troops.* Well, anyone reading that has some excuse for thinking that the British race is deteriorating!

As a matter of fact, it was the same sort of thing as here the 60,000 troops were there all right, spread over about eighty miles. I don't suppose there were more than sixty just where he broke through. It makes a difference! This would be the sort of thing that happened, and that we were expecting all the time: The line would be advancing, a man every thirty yards or so;

about 200 yards behind them would be a forlorn little mob of a couple of sections as support about every half-mile, and away to left or right- rear the convoy and main body. Of course, brother Joe would pick his place carefully. Probably you would be passing through bush, and perhaps approaching a little *kopje*, or farm with plenty of buildings.

When you were about one hundred yards from this (feeling pretty jumpy) there would come a volley, which with any luck would put about four of the line out of action, thus clearing a space of a couple of hundred yards. Friend Boer would then canter through. The forlorn little support would open out and hustle him a bit, but would have no time to hit more than five or six (and only that if the Boers were clumsy. As likely as not only the four who were hit saw them!).

CHAPTER 22

The End of the War

We went back to Klerksdorp after this, and found they were making preparations for a big drive, a lot of columns getting together near Klerksdorp, like they were when we came round from Volksrust. Some of our beauties began to get obstreperous here. It had been coming on ever since we joined the 27th, and came to a head the day we marched into Klerksdorp. My company had got a lot of wood just outside Klerksdorp (we always used to get as much wood as possible, going into a standing camp, for cooking), and were carrying it along, when the commanding-officer sent up to know:

Who gave us leave to get wood?—We were to drop it at once. Well, we dropped it all right, and it was immediately picked up by the company behind us (one of the original 27th), who were allowed to keep it. This "kind er riled" the bold Hampshires, and thenceforward they made a point of talking sedition, privy conspiracy, and rebellion, amongst themselves whenever an officer was in hearing. Tommy is a past master in the art of being mutinous in a way that you cannot "have" him for, and they made things pretty unpleasant.

Then they got some beer up to camp, and were going to make the men parade for it and drink it before an officer. The men said they paid for it, and if they couldn't drink it when they liked they wouldn't have it (a tremendous sacrifice this). So it was emptied out, and they wheeled the company in front of Lowe, who talked to us like a father. Three or four of the most "unreconcilable" were sent back to the regiment at Johannesburg ("Coffee" Oakford amongst them), and we returned to a certain amount of "good order and military discipline."

At last everything was ready, and we set out on the last drive of the war, straight across to the line from Kimberley to Mafeking. We must have covered a lot of country, for there were six or eight columns. Old Thorneycroft was on our right. About the fourth day out we were going through some bush, when a man on the flank of my section lost touch, and we got out of the line. We thought we were behind, and started trotting, with the result that when we reached open country no one else was in sight. We had been in front all the way, so we were liable to catch it, anyway.

Our line would take us for Boers and get the big guns on us, and the Boers would also mangle us if they came along. We had reached this decision, when a few Boers did "happen along" and sniped us persistently from the fringe of timber; but they did no damage, and presently we saw the line coming along far behind us.

There was a lieutenant with us—Mr. Earl[1]—and he called me up for a consultation. He was rather a character. He began: "That is our line."

"Yessir!"

"There is a flag."

"Yessir!"

"That flag belongs to a General Officer."

"Yessir!"

"That flag is to be avoided!"

So we did our damnedest to avoid that flag. We cut into the bush and rode obliquely along the line; but the line was wheeling, and we emerged not a hundred yards from the same flag-

---

1. There was a legend about Mr. Earl in the company. He was supposed at one time to be very sick of trekking; and one night he got outside the outpost line. The sentry challenged and snapped his breech-block to in an alarming manner (the shot was generally pretty quick after the challenge). But apparently Mr. Earl thought it would be just as well to get a spell in hospital. He only drawled: "All right, if you shoot, shoot me in the leg!"

Thorneycroft!!! He called Mr. Earl up, and I was thanking my stars that Mr, Earl had been with us, for I was second in command. However, he was in a good humour and only laughed, and we meandered off along the line to find Lowe's column.

The worst of this drive was want of water. We often had to ride eight or ten miles to water horses after getting into camp! And we were only allowed a pint a man from the water-carts. One day we heard we were getting to the Hart River, and were sure of a good drink—perhaps a wash; but the Hart River had left a *locum tenens* in the shape of one small muddy pool with about three very dead mules in it! This country is almost the Karroo, and the only living thing we saw were little silver foxes.

We saw no Boers till about the last day, though we got a lot of wagons that had been dragged right into the heart of thick bushes. We found the camp of this crowd behind a stone wall, and knew they had only just left (fires alight, etc.). I was in the support, and crossing a dry pan we suddenly saw about sixty or eighty gallop from behind some rocks towards a slight space between us and Thorneycroft.

We (the support) galloped for it, too, and got there first; so Joe went on and surrendered to Thorneycroft. Meanwhile, as the ground was rough and we couldn't see things well, we nearly had a spirited encounter with a mob sent by Thorneycroft for the same purpose as ours!

We went on to Vryburg then, still in line, and had quite a brisk engagement with the troops who were defending the line, armoured train and all! ! There was some excuse for them taking us for Boers, and we were not going to be fired at without retaliating; but I don't know why it was not stopped at once; I suppose they thought a few of us more or less made no difference! There was not much damage done, and our column camped at Vryburg. This was too sandy to be a pleasant camp.

We heard here that our old column (Pilcher's) had been distinguishing themselves again. They had gone into Kimberley. Now, the Munsters were stationed in Kimberley, and there was a company of Royal Irish in the 5th Mounted Infantry with

Pilcher, and the Mounted Infantry wore side-arms in town! Anyone who knows the standing feud between the two regiments will understand what happened. It began in the theatre. The Munsters' garrison police, glad of the chance, began "running in" some R.I. "insurgents." The Royal Irish rallied round these men, and the rest of the column rallied round the R.I. Sixteen dead and wounded was the result. I tell the yarn as we got it; it may have been exaggerated.

After a few days we drove back again to Klerksdorp, nothing of interest occurring except that we passed over two of Methuen's old battle-grounds and got a few odd Boers. In Klerksdorp they picked out the men to go home for the Coronation. If I had not got to be sergeant I should have gone, for I was the longest trekking corporal in the company, being the only one left of the original lot; but, of course, I was the junior sergeant, and two or three sergeants had been trekking all the time, too.

The Peace proclamation was read out on Church Parade, and we gave the regulation cheers. I don't know that I was much elated, though, on the whole; we had had a pretty good time all round, and would never probably get the same experiences again.

And now began a most unsatisfactory time, as a break-up always is. Regiments we knew and liked were going home to their respective colonies to be disbanded; Mounted Infantry regiments would rejoin their respective line battalions; troops would be hurried home to India. It was worse than the break-up of the holidays, as there was no chance of getting together again. My company was to track to Krugersdorp up the line (in advance of the regiment); and you cannot imagine the desolation one felt trekking along, a forlorn little mob with no flankers out! The knowledge that no one would shoot at us from the next skyline made us feel quite neglected.

At Krugersdorp we camped, and I began to wonder what I had better do. I wanted to get on the S.A.C., and everyone was too busy here to do anything; so at last I brought myself to apply for leave to rejoin the regiment (Hampshire) at Johannesburg.

My captain at this time was not much struck with me, strange to say, and made no objection. So I handed over the old mare (I had not had her long enough to care much) and my saddlery, and was duly struck off the strength of the Mounted Infantry. That night all my company sergeants, together with myself, went out in town, and the place was alive with Delarey's and Kemp's men coming in off commando, hobnobbing with Tommy in a most sociable way—men of every nationality, including, by their accent, Americans and English.

They were pretty rough when they came in—some dressed in buckskins of their own manufacture—but most had a couple of ponies, which they sold, and then they turned out with jackboots, feathered hats, etc., and generally spoilt their workmanlike looks. We went into an eating-house for supper, and a youngster at the next table, an awful-looking little bounder in flannel trousers and tennis shoes, striped linen shirt, and a little grocer's boy sort of collar, a narrow-rimmed straw hat, and a very pimply face, after looking at our helmet badge said, "Do you belong to the 27th Mounted Infantry?"

We admitted it. "Ah," he drawled, trying to twirl his moustache, "I captured one of your men the other day, name of Sharpe!" This was the chap they got on the night march, and made ride on the gun while they were dodging us.

JUST IN   HOPING THEY'LL TAKE HIM
                 FOR DELAREY!

This youngster told us all about it, and got very friendly. He was an American, who had been in the Staats Artillery all through the war. He told us that only about thirty of his lot wanted to keep on fighting, and he was one; of course, we only had his word for it. He condescended to come to the concert hall, where there was an entertainment of sorts, and pointed out the Boers of note; the place was full of these.

Next day I and another fellow who was going back to the Regiment (a Corporal Hill, signaller), shouldered our kits and cleared off to Johannesburg by rail. We took an open cab, and flashed up through Johannesburg to a restaurant for lunch, and then off up to the Fort (the fort that Kruger built to overawe the Johannesburgers). The first person I saw was "Coffee" Oakford on sentry at the main gate! He gave us a look as much as to say, "You're out of the frying-pan into the fire! "and the return to barrack life, after the open-air life of the *veldt*, was so marked that it was almost like enlisting again.

Well, that's the end of the war, so I can dry up; but I must end up with a few appropriately sentimental reflections; all the best authors do. Stand by!

So ends the great struggle between Briton and Boer; and as we sit and ponder over the events of those stirring years, what visions, grave and gay, will float before our eyes in the changing smoke wreaths! (I don't smoke, but keep it dark.) Shall we not see again the mounted column rolling o'er the boundless plain,

ONE OF DELAREY'S *DESPERADOES* AFTER PEACE

228

in the dim misty morning twilight, and hear in imagination the muttered "'nother b——y night march"?

But, alas, never again will our souls be stirred by the clarion call, ringing down the horse-lines, "Rum up"; never again (thank God) shall we be roused at 2 a.m. by a kick in the back and "Get these feeds on." No more shall we sit on hard antheaps in a broiling sun, stripped to the waist as heroes fought in Nelson's day, the while we chase the homely but elusive louse through the intricacies of a grey-back shirt. No, these things are of the past; and we who have turned our swords into ploughshares (I've done better than most, I changed a bayonet with a broken spring into a four-furrow disc plough!) will come in time to look upon them as strange dreams, that, passing through our waking thoughts, provoke the smile or sigh. (How's that? eh, what?)

BEFORE PEACE

"SWORDS INTO PLOUGHSHARES"

www.ingramcontent.com/pod-product-compliance
Lightning Source LLC
Chambersburg PA
CBHW032050080426
42733CB00006B/224